THE SERIOUS GUITARIST
ROCK CHOPS

A technique-building approach
for the dedicated guitarist

Tobias Hurwitz

ABOUT THE MP3 CD

The included CD features audio recordings for the exercises in the book. Listening to the recordings will help you accurately interpret the feel and rhythm for each exercise.

Instructions

To access the MP3 files, place the disc in the CD drive of your computer.

Windows users: Double-click on My Computer, right-click on your CD drive icon, select Explore, and then double-click on *The Serious Guitarist Rock Chops MP3s* folder.

Mac users: Double-click on the CD icon on your desktop, and then double-click on the *The Serious Guitarist Rock Chops MP3s* folder.

Alfred Music
P.O. Box 10003
Van Nuys, CA 91410-0003
alfred.com

ISBN-10: 0-7390-9305-3 (Book & CD)
ISBN-13: 978-0-7390-9305-4 (Book & CD)

Cover photo by Tim Becker, Creative Image Photography, Manchester, CT

Alfred Cares. Contents printed on environmentally responsible paper.

CONTENTS

INTRODUCTION

There's a certain kind of person who's driven to play powerful, aggressive, rock 'n' roll lead guitar. If that describes you, then you've come to the right place. Whether you're interested in just jamming, shredding, rocking out, or soul searching with the knobs set to "11," this book is designed to help you meet your goals. To get the most of this book, you should already have the basics mastered, including note names and music reading, tablature, scale forms, basic technique, and some theory. If you need a review on these topics, Chapter 1: Using This Book, starting on page 5, and Chapter 22: Scale Forms, starting on page 72, will be helpful. You should familiarize yourself with those sections first.

This book covers intermediate and advanced techniques such as sweep picking, tremolo picking, alternate picking, economy picking, whammy bar, finger tapping, string skipping, legato, artificial harmonics, linking arpeggios, exotic scales, long scales, and more. So get ready to dig into a boat-load of cool practice material. This book presents all of the most interesting lead guitar secrets I've come across over a lifetime of studying rock lead guitar. Your playing will surely improve as you add these exciting techniques to your arsenal.

Go get 'em!

Tobias Hurwitz

Track 1 will help you tune to this CD.

ABOUT THE AUTHOR

GIT grad Tobias Hurwitz has devoted his life to playing and teaching guitar. He has authored the ever-popular method book, *The Total Rock Guitarist*, and 14 more books with Alfred Music. Hurwitz is widely published by trade journals such as *Guitar Player*, *Guitar*, and *Guitar One* magazines. His discography includes three solo releases and many collaborations, most recently on Michael Angelo Batio's *Intermezzo* release, where he shares album credits with the likes of Guthrie Govan, Rusty Cooley, George Lynch, and Chris Poland (formerly of Megadeth).

Named "Baltimore's Best Guitar Teacher," Tobias Hurwitz teaches guitar at home, via Skype, at Hagerstown Community College, and on TrueFire.com. He has over a million YouTube views and plays live in various settings, including The Baltimore Ravens Rhythm Section, where he plays to a stadium crowd eight times a year.

Tobias is endorsed by: Paul Reed Smith Guitars, Ernie Ball Strings, and Fractal Audio.

Visit www.tobiashurwitz.com

Tobias would like to thank his friends, family and fellow musicians who have encouraged him over the years, and the editors at Alfred Music for their hard work.

CHAPTER 1: HOW TO USE THIS BOOK

Scale Diagrams

The top line of a scale diagram represents the 1st (highest) string of the guitar, and the bottom line is the 6th (lowest) string. The vertical lines represent frets which are numbered.

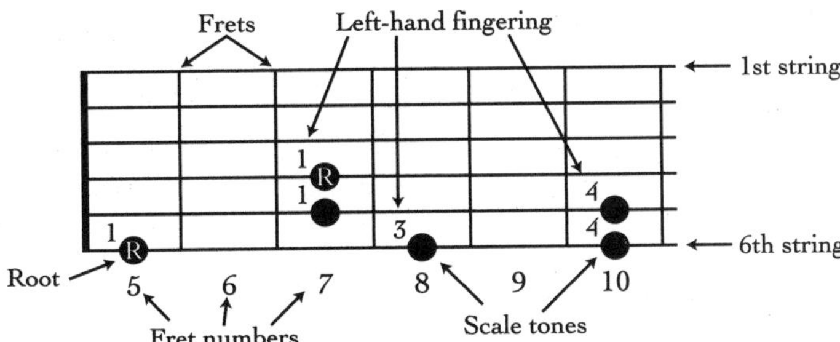

Reading Tablature (TAB)

Tablature, also known as TAB, is a means of notating the exact location of notes on the fretboard. The six lines correspond directly to the six strings of the guitar. The numbers on the lines indicate the frets that the left-hand fingers play.

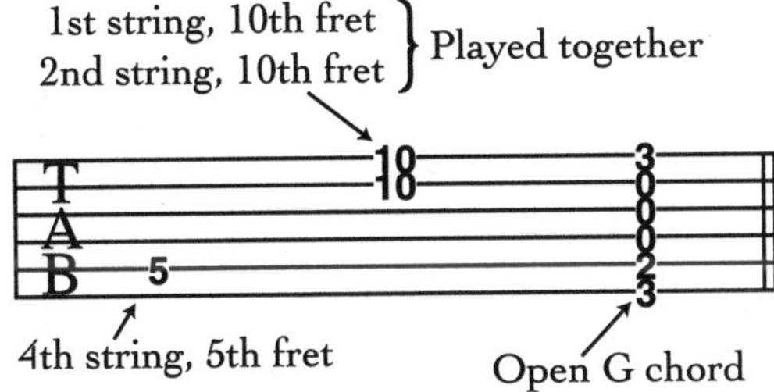

Special Notation

In our system of tablature, we use special markings to indicate techniques like bends, slides, hammers, pull-offs, and harmonics. Upward bends are marked with an upward arrow. Downward arrows are used to show a bend release. A number above the arrow tells how far the note is to be bent (1 = one whole step, ½ = one half step, etc.). A slanted line with an "S" above it indicates a slide. A hammer-on or pull-off is indicated by a curved line with an "H" or "P" above it. The abbreviation "Nat. Harm." means "natural harmonic." "Art. Harm." means "artificial harmonic." These and other symbols are shown in examples starting on page 6–7.

Examples of Special TAB Notation

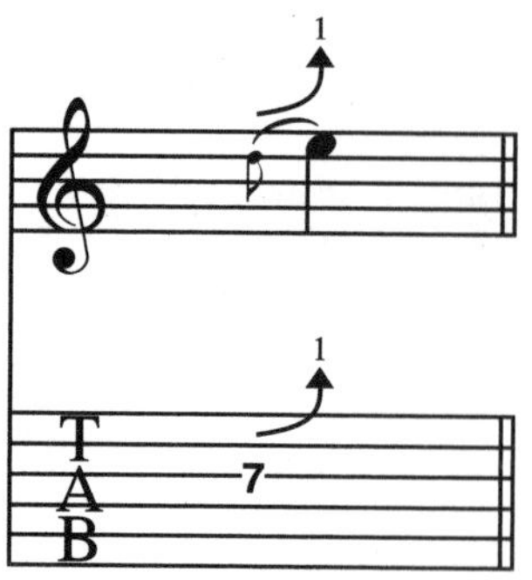

Bend

Strike the note and bend it up one whole step (the sound of the note two frets above the starting pitch). Notice the use of a *grace note* (a small, quick, decorative note). Bend notation also includes a *slur*. With a slur, only the first note is plucked.

Bend and Release

Bend the first note as indicated. Then, release it back to the original note in the rhythm shown. Only the first note is plucked.

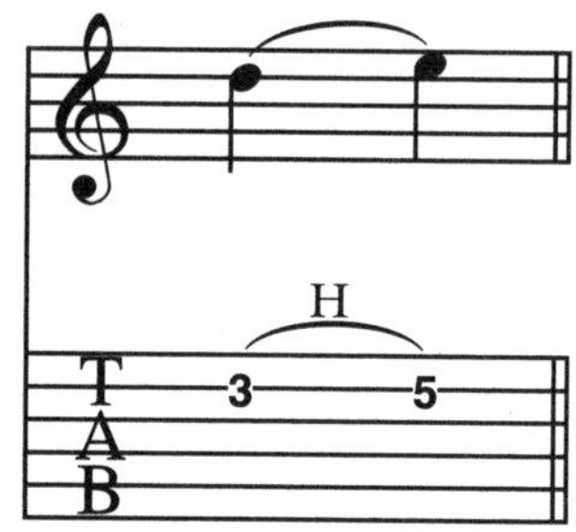

Hammer-On

Hammer-ons are indicated with a slur. Strike the first note, then slam a left-hand finger down so that the second (higher) note sounds without being plucked.

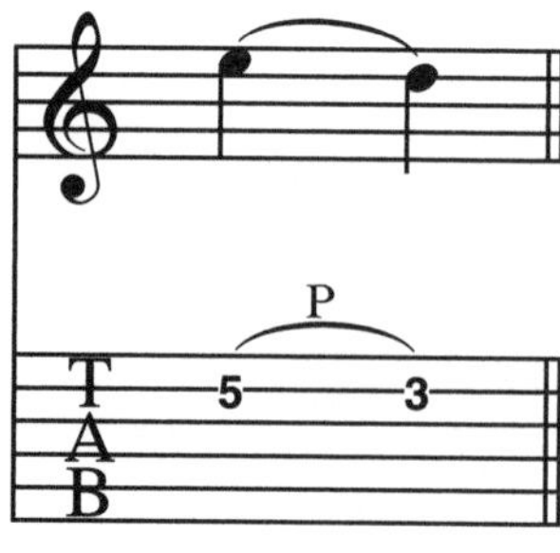

Pull-Off

Pull-offs are indicated with a slur. Put both fingers on the notes to be played. Strike the first note, then pull that finger down (towards the floor) so that the second note sounds without being plucked.

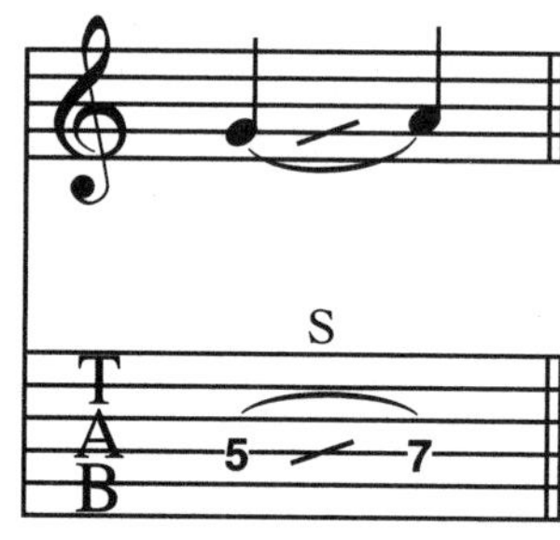

Slide

Strike the first note, then slide the finger along the string to the second note. Do not strike the second note.

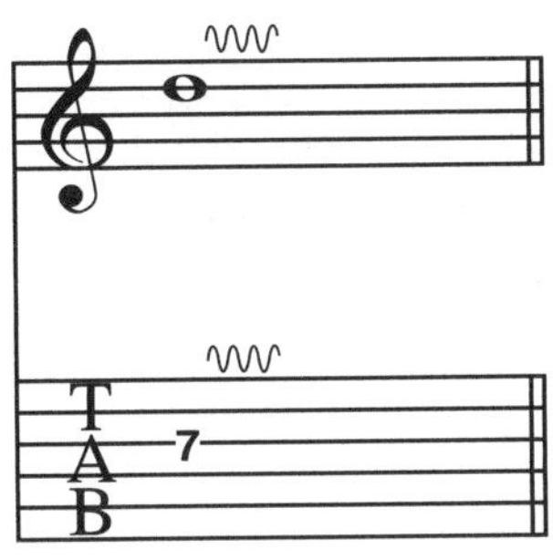

Vibrato

Rapidly bend and release the note with the left hand or whammy bar to create an expressive, vocal, vibrating sound.

Palm Muting

The right hand lightly touches the string just next to the bridge producing a slightly dampened sound.

Tapping

Sound the notes by hammering-on with a right-hand finger.

m =	Tap with the middle finger of the right hand.
i =	Tap with the index finger of the right hand.

Natural Harmonic

The string is struck while the left-hand finger lightly touches directly over the indicated fret.

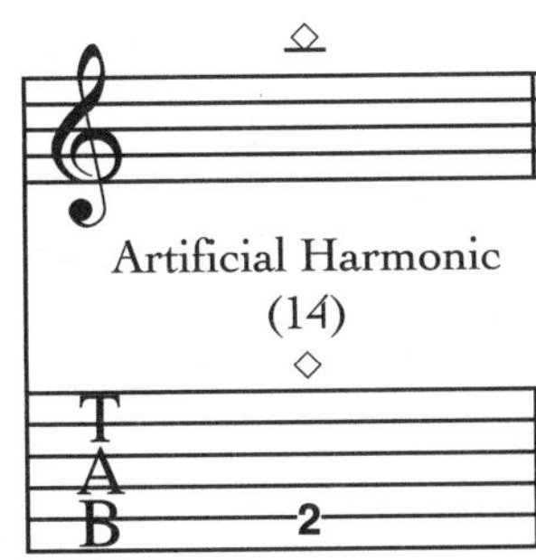

Artificial Harmonic

The note is fretted normally. The harmonic is produced by striking the string with the side of the thumb, or a fingertip, in conjunction with the pick at the fret shown in parentheses above the TAB.

CHAPTER 2: DON'T HURT YOURSELF

Many guitarists experience hand problems of one kind or another at various times in their careers. These problems are often the result of practicing too much or with bad technique. The purpose of this section is to help you avoid these frustrating pitfalls or learn to live with an existing hand problem. Here are some dos and don'ts.

Do:

- Stretch and warm up before practicing or performing.

- Try to keep your wrists as straight as possible while playing.

- If you already have a problem, consult your physician about anti-inflammatories such as ibuprofen. It may be helpful to take these prior to playing a lot or very rigorously.

Don't:

- Continue to play if it hurts.

- Press unnecessarily hard on the strings.

- Play with technique that causes your wrists to be bent more than necessary.

Stretching the Wrists

Put your palms together as if you were praying. Slowly lower your arms and put your elbows out, bending your wrists, so that you feel a stretch in your wrist tendons (see Figure A). When you feel a comfortable (not painful) level of stretching, hold that position for about one minute.

Figure A. Stretching the wrists.

Now, slowly rotate your wrists forward, so that your fingers point away from your body (see Figure B). This will cause the stretching sensation to move farther up into your forearms. Again, find a comfortable stretch that does not hurt and hold it for a minute or so.

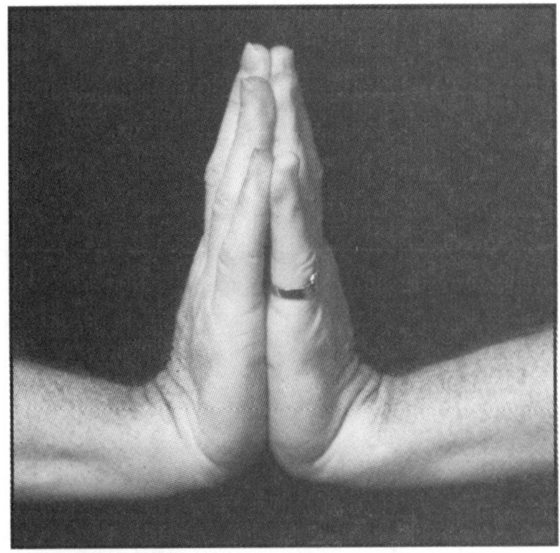

Figure B. Rotate the wrists forward.

Stretching the Fingers

Individually bend each finger back with the palm of your other hand (see Figure C). Find a comfortable, non-painful stretch. Hold the stretch for thirty seconds or so. Repeat on all fingers of both hands.

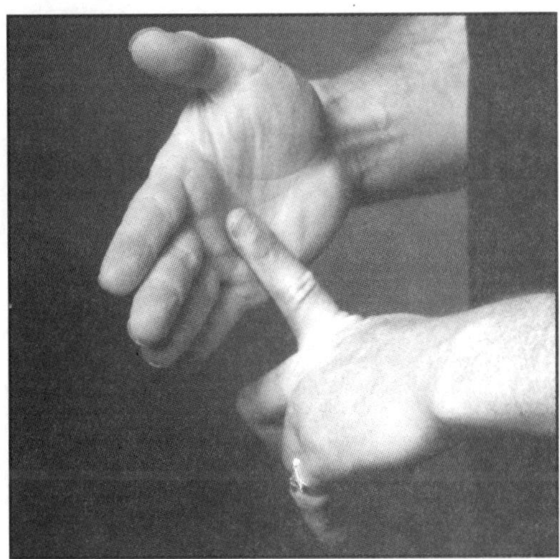

Figure C. Bend each finger back.

The Importance of Straight Wrists

Many hand problems, such as *tendonitis* (an inflammation of the tendons), can be caused by tendons rubbing together. The more rubbing the tendons do, the more they become inflamed, even scarred, causing them to rub even more severely.

Try this simple experiment: Extend both hands in front of your body without holding a guitar. Keep your wrists straight and move your fingers about, as if you were playing a rapid scale passage. You will find that there is very little tension in your wrist tendons. Now, while continuing to move your fingers, bend your wrists. You will find that the more you bend your wrists toward a right angle, the more difficult it becomes to move your fingers. The further you bend, the more excess tension you feel. To play with as little excess tension as possible and preserve the health of your tendons, it is important to keep the wrists as straight as possible. We all know that it is impossible to maintain an absolutely straight wrist while playing guitar. Playing certain barre chords, scale passages, etc. require the wrists to be bent. Just do the best you can.

To recap: Stretch and warm up before playing. Take breaks. Don't continue to play if it hurts. Don't press harder than necessary, and try to keep both wrists as straight as possible. If you follow this advice, you will stand a much better chance of remaining free of any serious hand problems. Now go shred in good health.

CHAPTER 3: ALTERNATE PICKING

Alternate picking is arguably the most common and effective method of picking. It consists of moving down and up with the pick, and never repeating two of the same strokes in a row. Grasp the pick between your thumb and first finger as shown in the photograph below. This is the "pro" grip and works well for alternate picking as well as all of the other techniques in this book. You should either pick from the wrist or the arm. Neither method is better and both should be learned so that you can choose which is best for any given situation. Picking from the wrist should be achieved by making small down and up motions. When picking from the arm, the wrist stays mostly locked in place, and the picking motion originates from the elbow. Extreme speed and fluidity is possible with either technique.

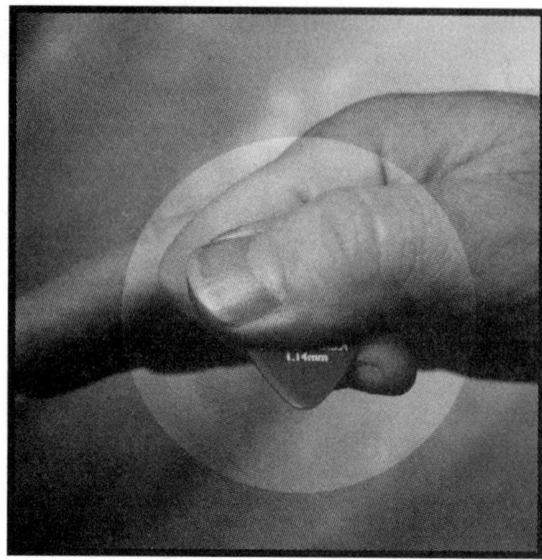

Pick grip

This first exercise will get you started alternate picking different rhythms on one string.

⊓ = *Downstroke*. Pick down towards the floor.

∨ = *Upstroke*. Pick up towards the ceiling.

> = *Accent*. Emphasize the note.

Exercise 1

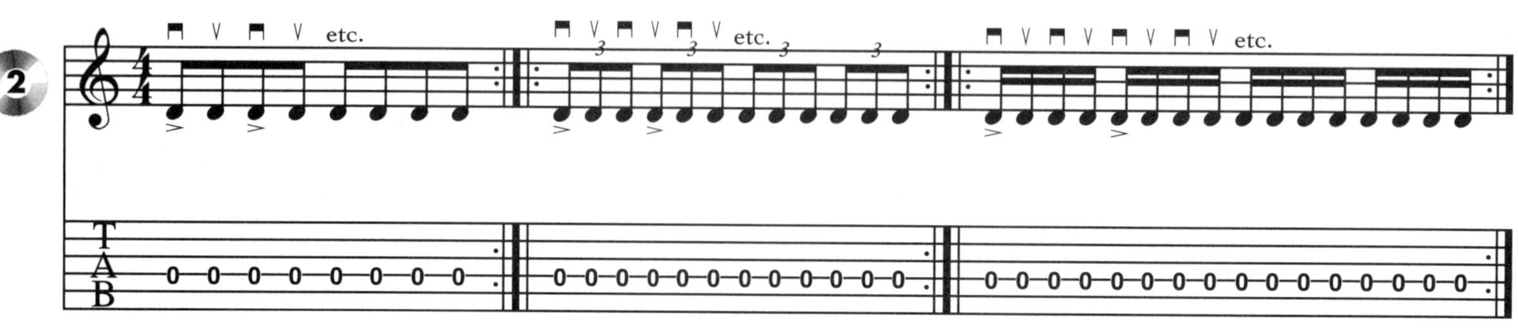

The next group of exercises introduces *string shifting*. String shifting is changing from one string to another. Notice how the "inside" shift, one where we change to a higher string on a downstroke, is harder than the "outside" shift, one where we change to a higher string on an upstroke. Notice also how the string-skipping shift is harder than the adjacent string shift. It is important to be aware of string shifting and to consciously practice the different shifts.

Exercise 2

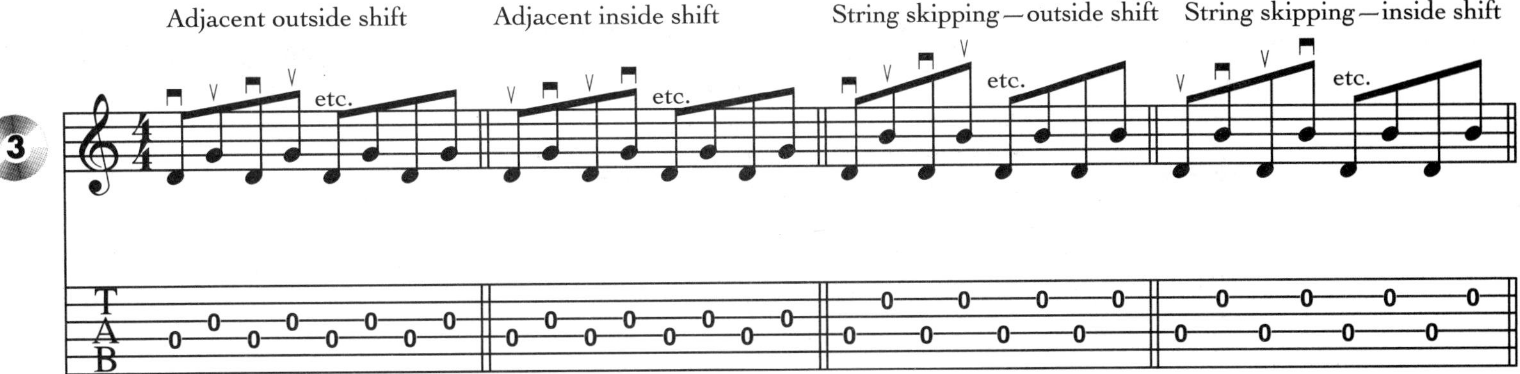

This simple pentatonic phrase features only the outside shift. If you start with an upstroke instead of a downstroke, only the inside shift will be featured. You should practice it both ways.

Exercise 3

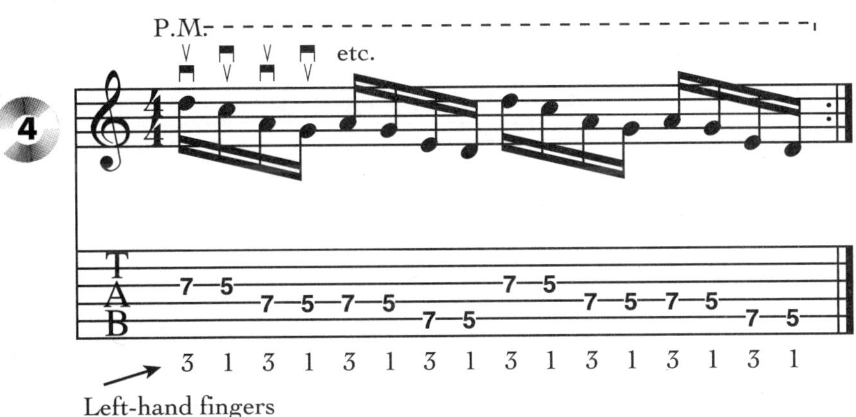

This three-note-per-string major scale is a great drill. Notice how the inside and outside shifts alternate as you move across the strings. Notice the *sextuplet* rhythm — six notes in the time of four.

Exercise 4

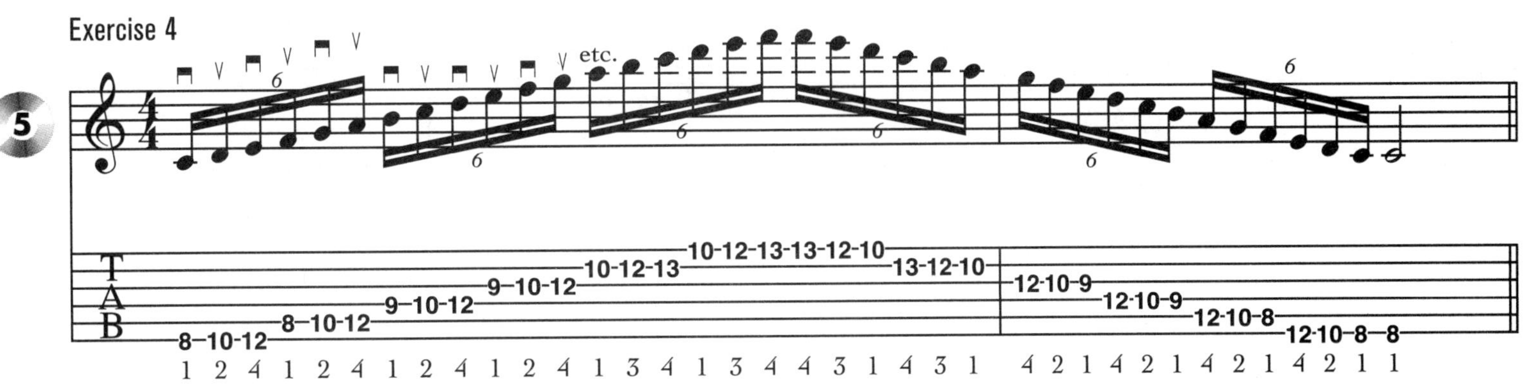

This three-note pattern scale study features only the inside shift. If you start with an upstroke instead of a downstroke, only the outside shift will be featured. You should practice it both ways.

Exercise 5

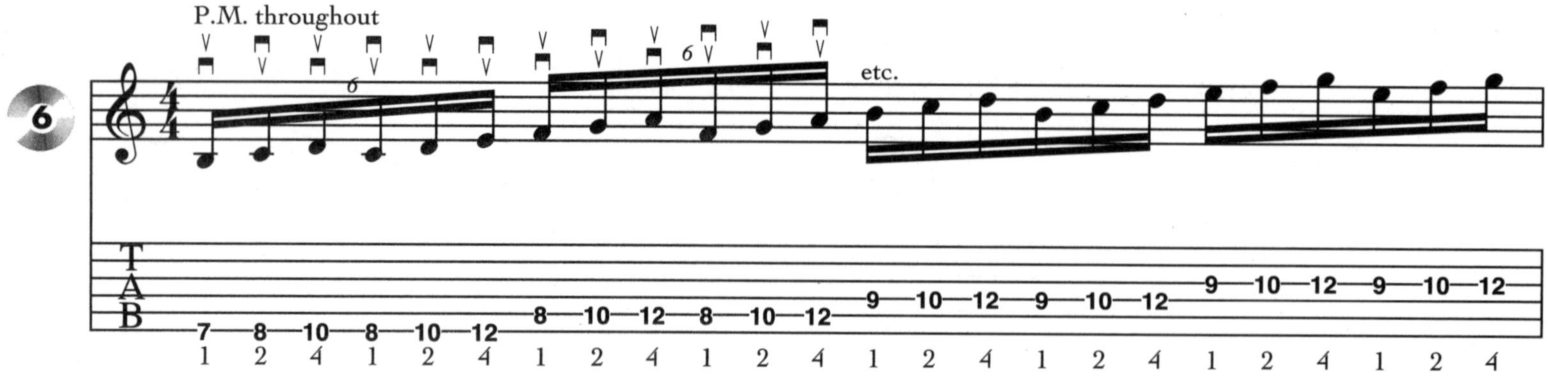

8va- - - = *Ottava.* Play an octave higher or lower than the notes written.

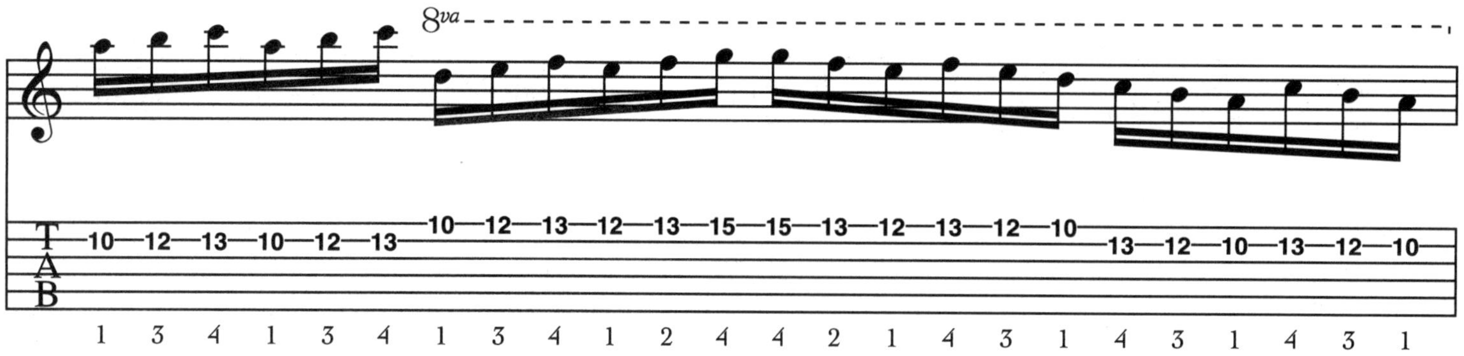

This diminished scale study is another excellent chops builder. The exotic sounds of the
diminished scale are more fully explained in the Exotic Scales section on page 55. This exercise
is written in *quintuplets*—five notes in the time of four.

Exercise 6

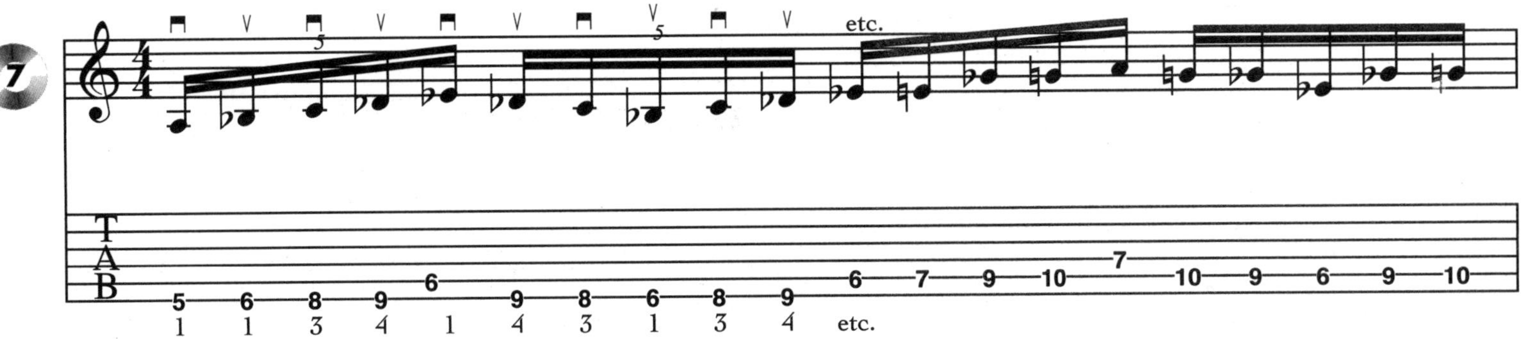

CHAPTER 4: ECONOMY PICKING

Economy picking is a highly efficient method of picking in which the pick follows the path of least resistance. It is very closely related to *sweep picking* (page 16) but applies to scales as well as arpeggios. With economy picking, if you move down a string (toward the floor) then you play a downstroke and if you move up (toward the ceiling) then you play an upstroke. For any notes that are on the same string you simply alternate pick. Many players fall into economy picking by accident while attempting to alternate pick. This is because they fail to notice that the pick has gone down twice in a row or up twice in a row while shifting from one string to another.

The following example is an economy-picked three-note-per-string A Dorian scale. Notice how the pick executes two consecutive downstrokes to shift from string to string while ascending, and two consecutive upstrokes to shift while descending.

Exercise 7

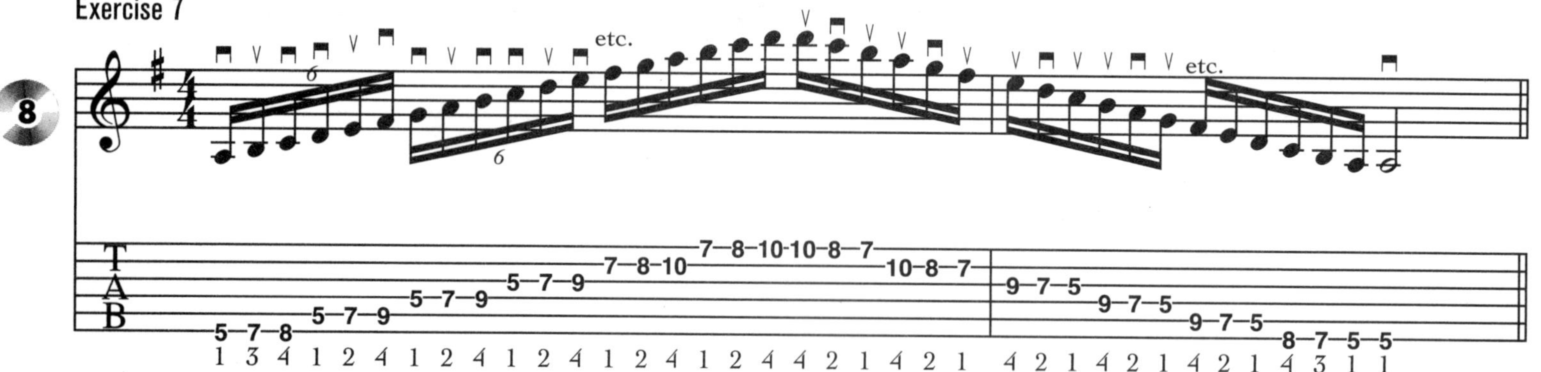

Here's a smokin' A Minor rock 'n' roll riff that uses economy picking.

Exercise 8

Here's a more advanced version of the riff in Example 8. It combines economy picking and *finger tapping* (page 42). Finger tap the 17th fret of the 1st string with your right-hand 2nd finger (*i*).

Exercise 9

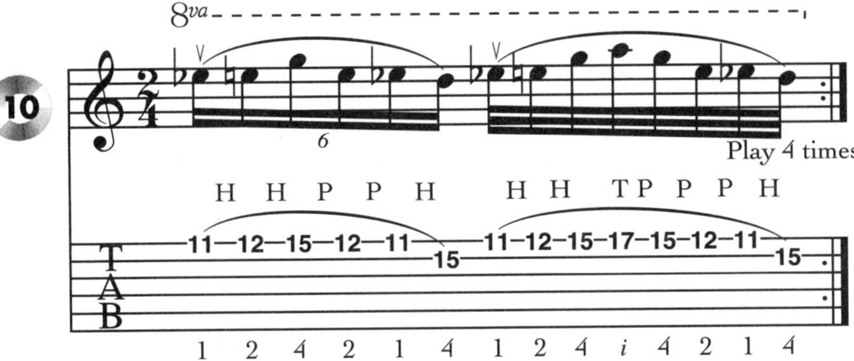

This C Major scale study *sequences* (see page 33) a melodic fragment from J. S. Bach's *Double Violin Concerto in D Minor*. It is a perfect example of economy picking and a great chops builder.

Exercise 10

CHAPTER 5: SWEEP PICKING

Sweep picking is a technique used by players like Yngwie Malmsteen and Frank Gambale to play arpeggios with extreme speed and fluidity. In sweeping, the right hand plays three or more of the same picking strokes in a row (all down or all up), while the left hand plays one note per string. The right hand "strums" smoothly down and up, while the left hand tracks each pick attack with a single note. Sometimes there is a hammer-on or pull-off that "turns around" the arpeggio. When playing these examples, it is very important to pay attention to the indicated pick strokes. It is also important to pick from the arm and smoothly connect each stroke, rather than individually picking each note from the wrist.

This first example is an A Minor 7 arpeggio and is a comparatively easy way to get started sweeping.

Exercise 11

Playing the same shape starting on the 4th string creates a dominant 7 arpeggio.

Exercise 12

This exercise uses the arpeggios from Examples 11 and 12 to form a big loop. It is entirely in the key of C Major and begins on G7, the V chord of the key. The ii, iii, and vi chords are also represented. This is a great tool for beginning to work sweeping into your improvisation.

Exercise 13

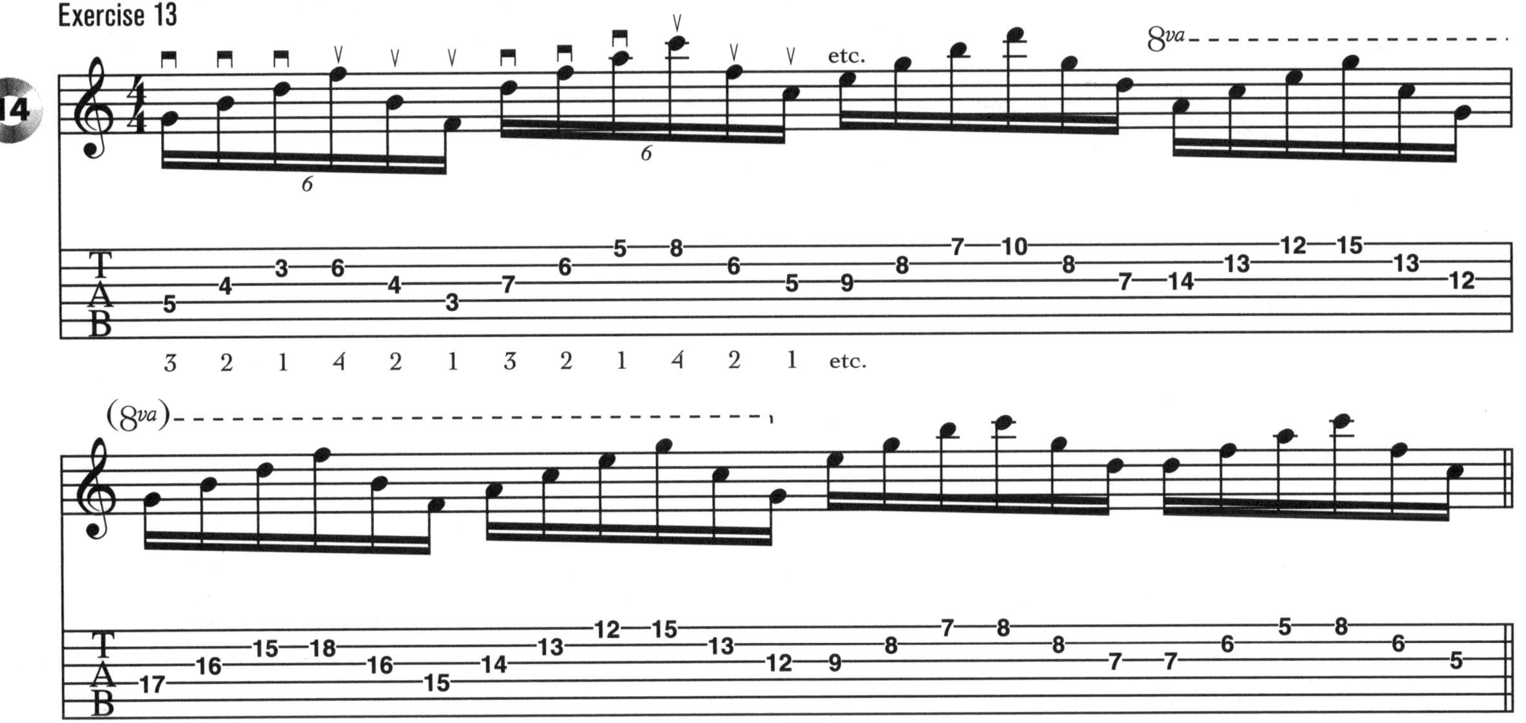

This cool sweep ascends through the F Major 7th arpeggio and descends through its relative minor arpeggio, D Minor.

Exercise 14

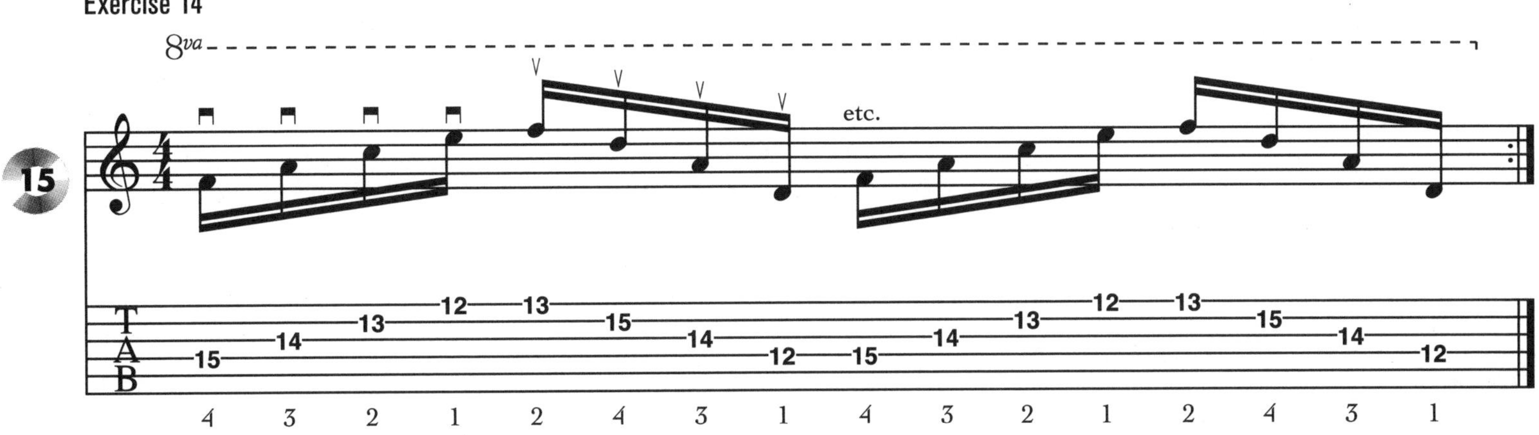

This lick expands the previous idea by sliding around to more arpeggios, which are all in the key of C Major.

Exercise 15

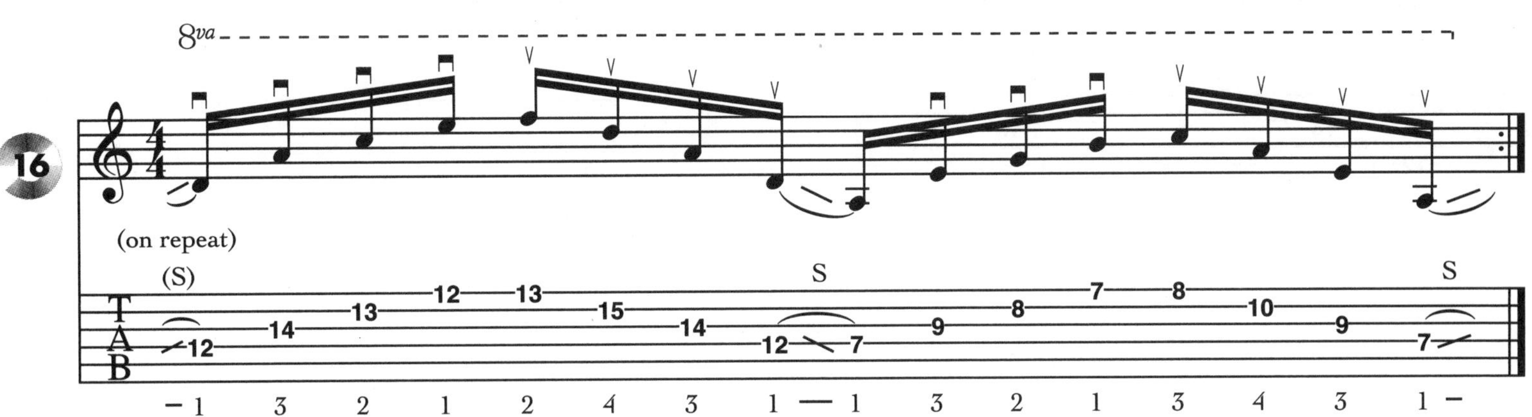

Here are more arpeggio forms for practicing sweep picking:

Exercise 16

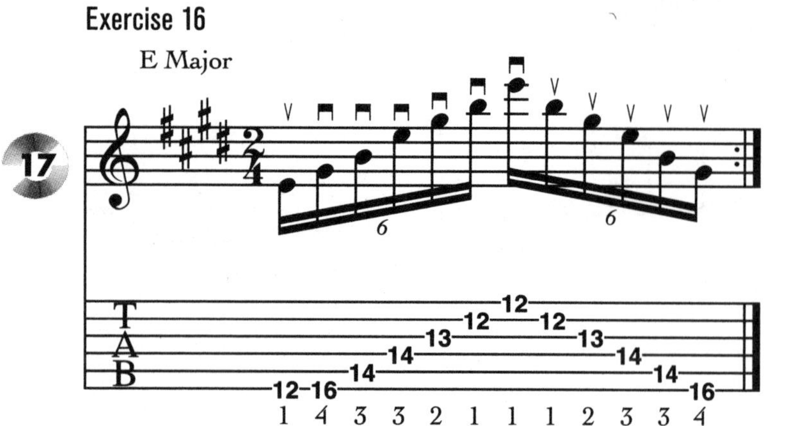

Exercise 17

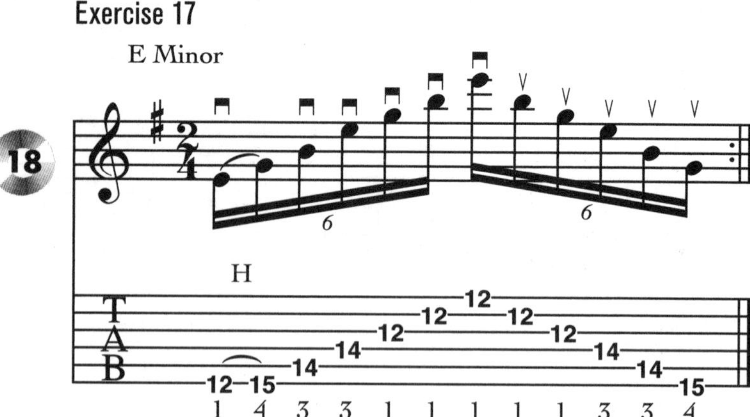

Exercise 18

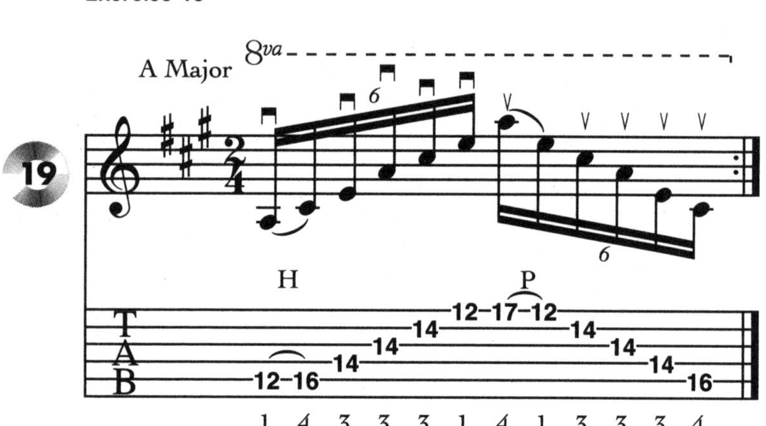

Exercise 19

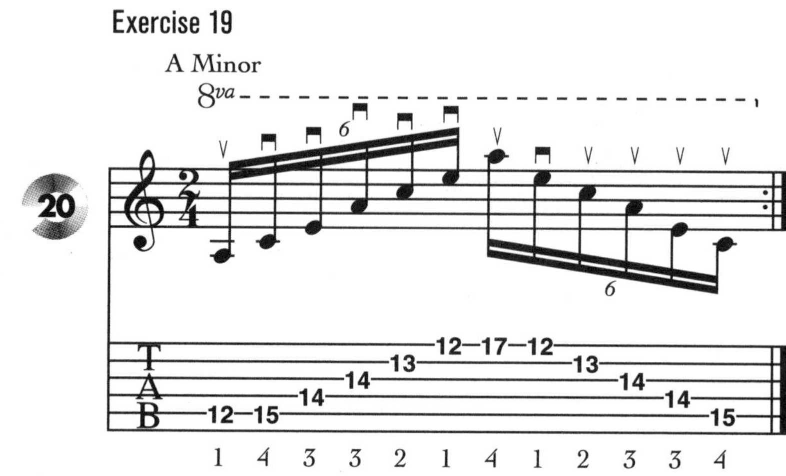

Exercise 20

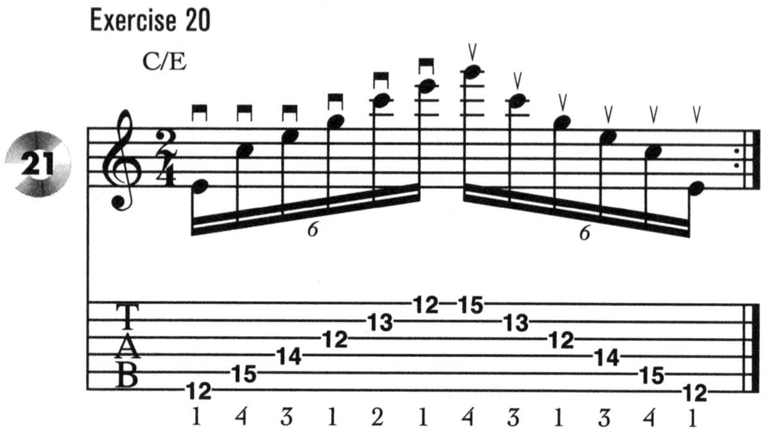

Exercise 21

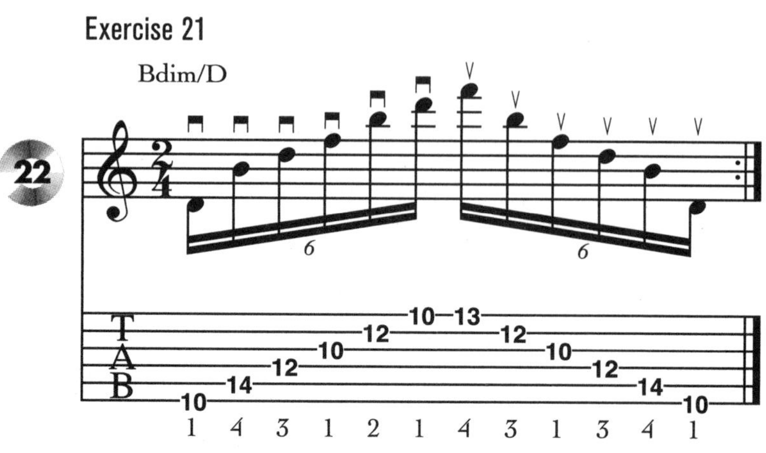

This example links two diatonic arpeggios: C/E and Bdim/D. For more of this sort of playing, see
the arpeggio etudes section (page 63).

Exercise 22

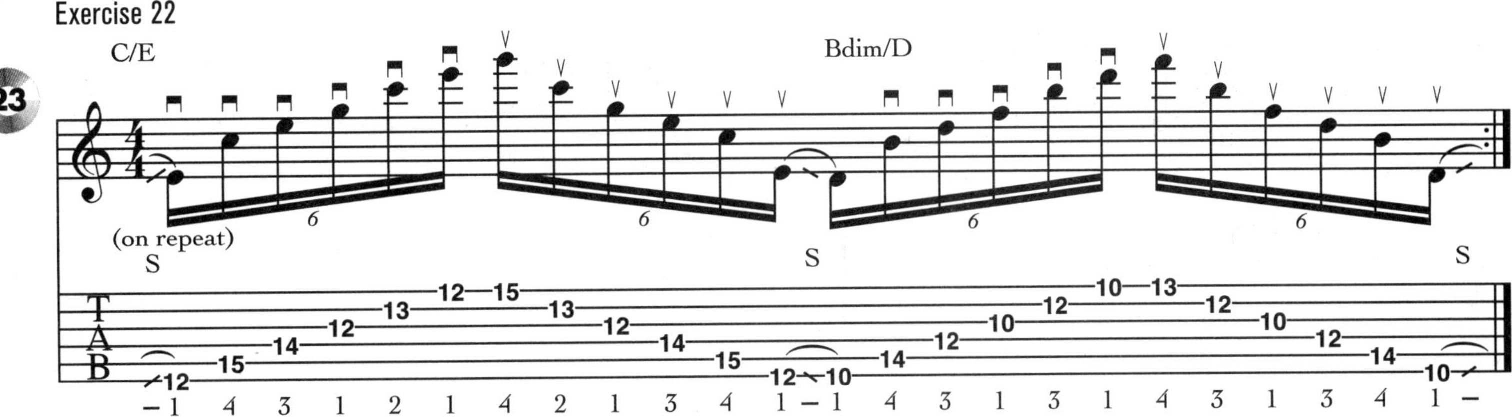

The B Diminished 7 arpeggio is inverted three times and looped in Example 23, which is in the
style of Yngwie Malmsteen.

Exercise 23

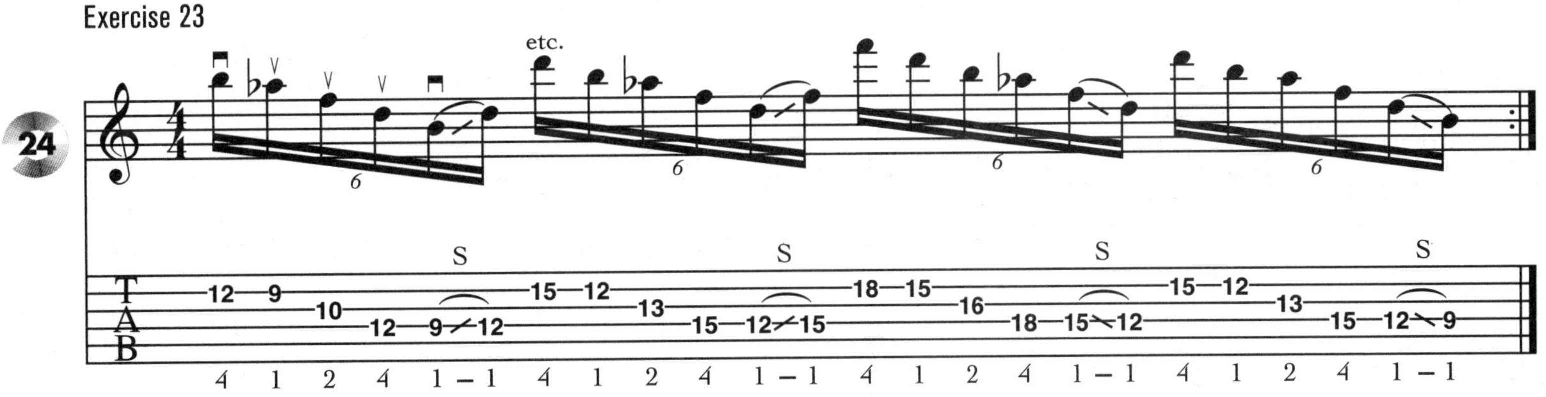

This D Diminished arpeggio sequence will burn up your neck, in the shredding syle of Yngwie
Malmsteen.

Exercise 24

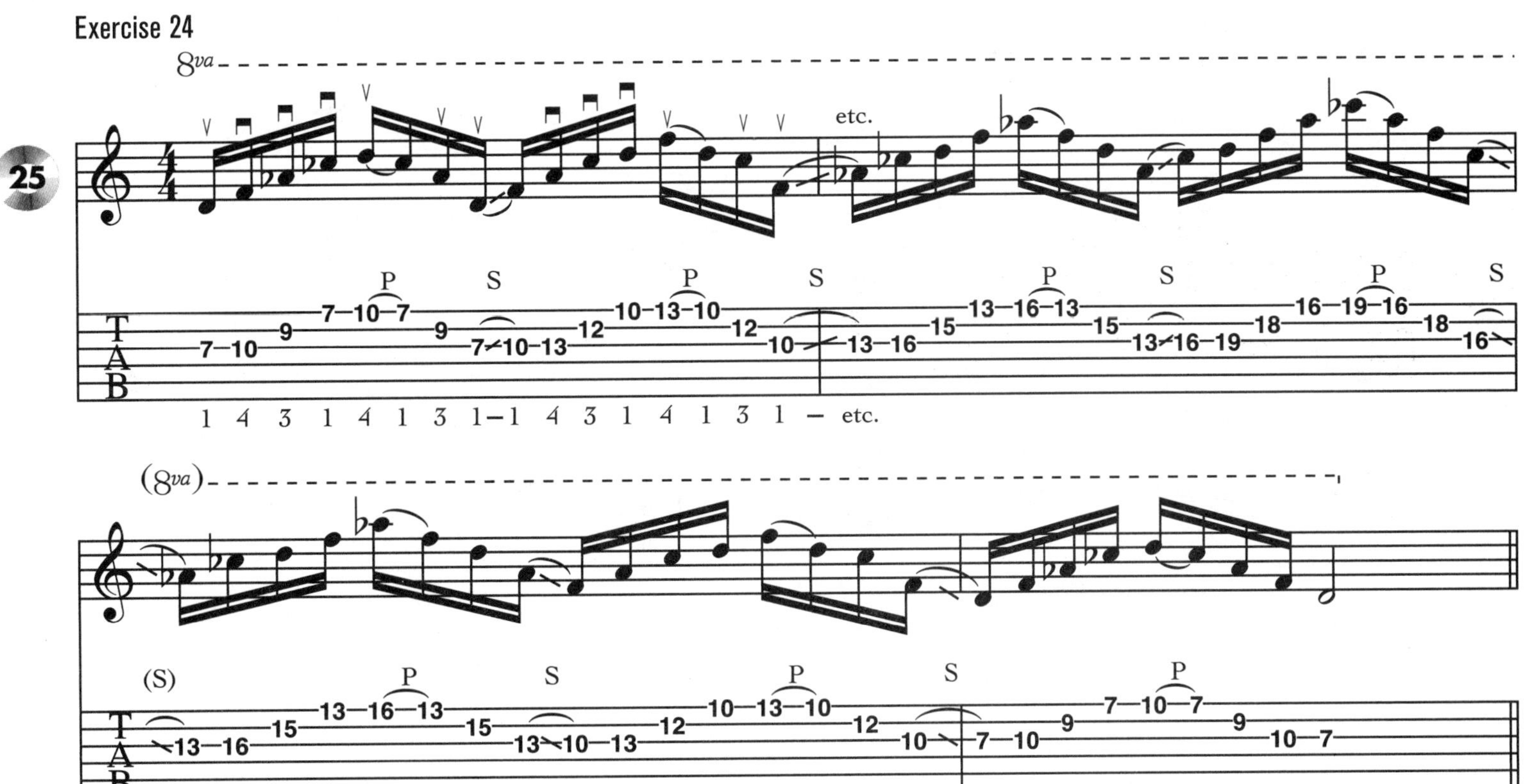

Once you have mastered a few arpeggio forms, you may wish to begin applying them by outlining chord progressions with arpeggios. The following two examples show how this can be done.

Exercise 25 outlines a I–IV–V–IV progression in C Major.

Exercise 25

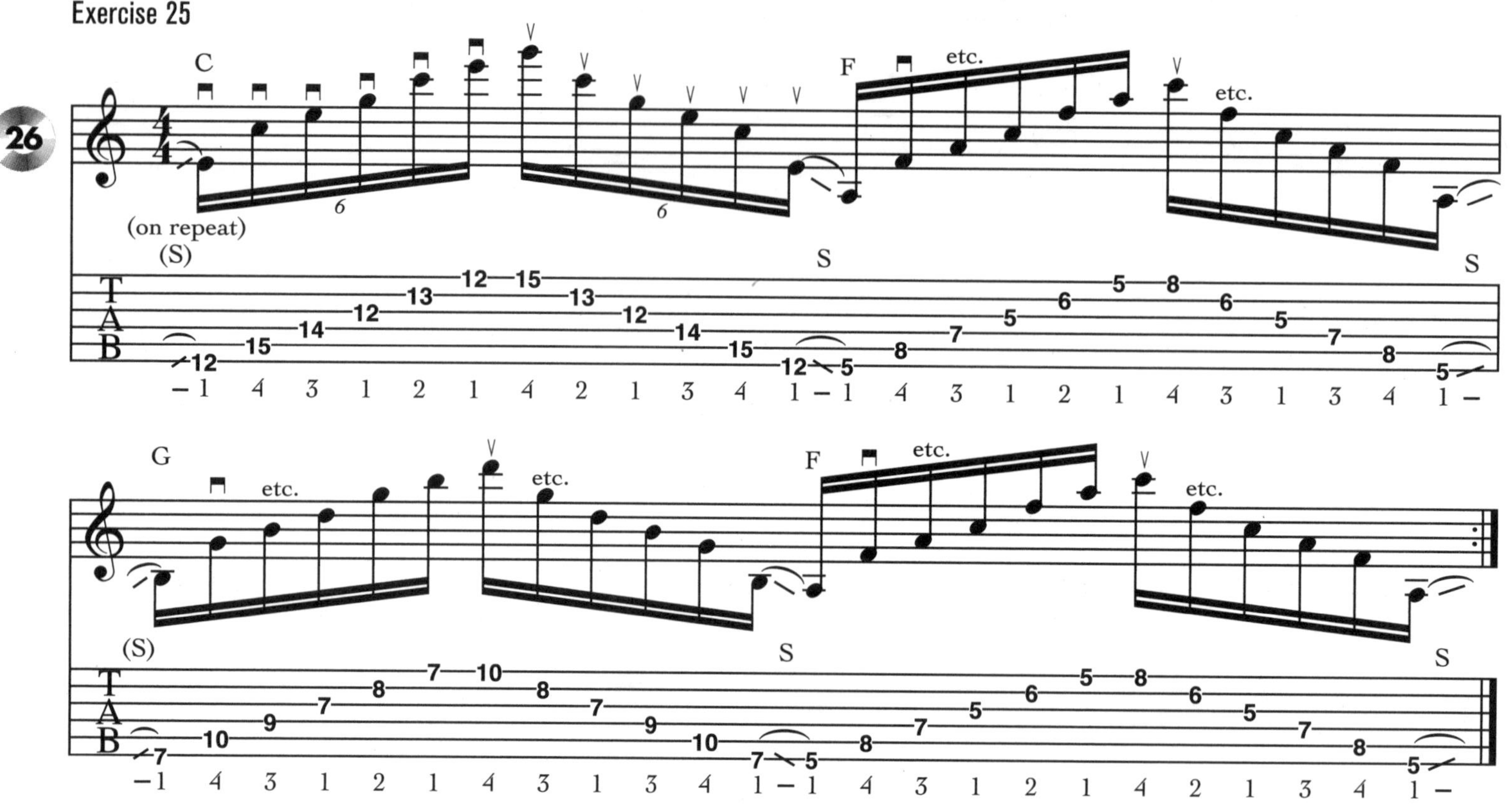

Exercise 26 outlines a IV–V–vi–I progression in D Major.

Exercise 26

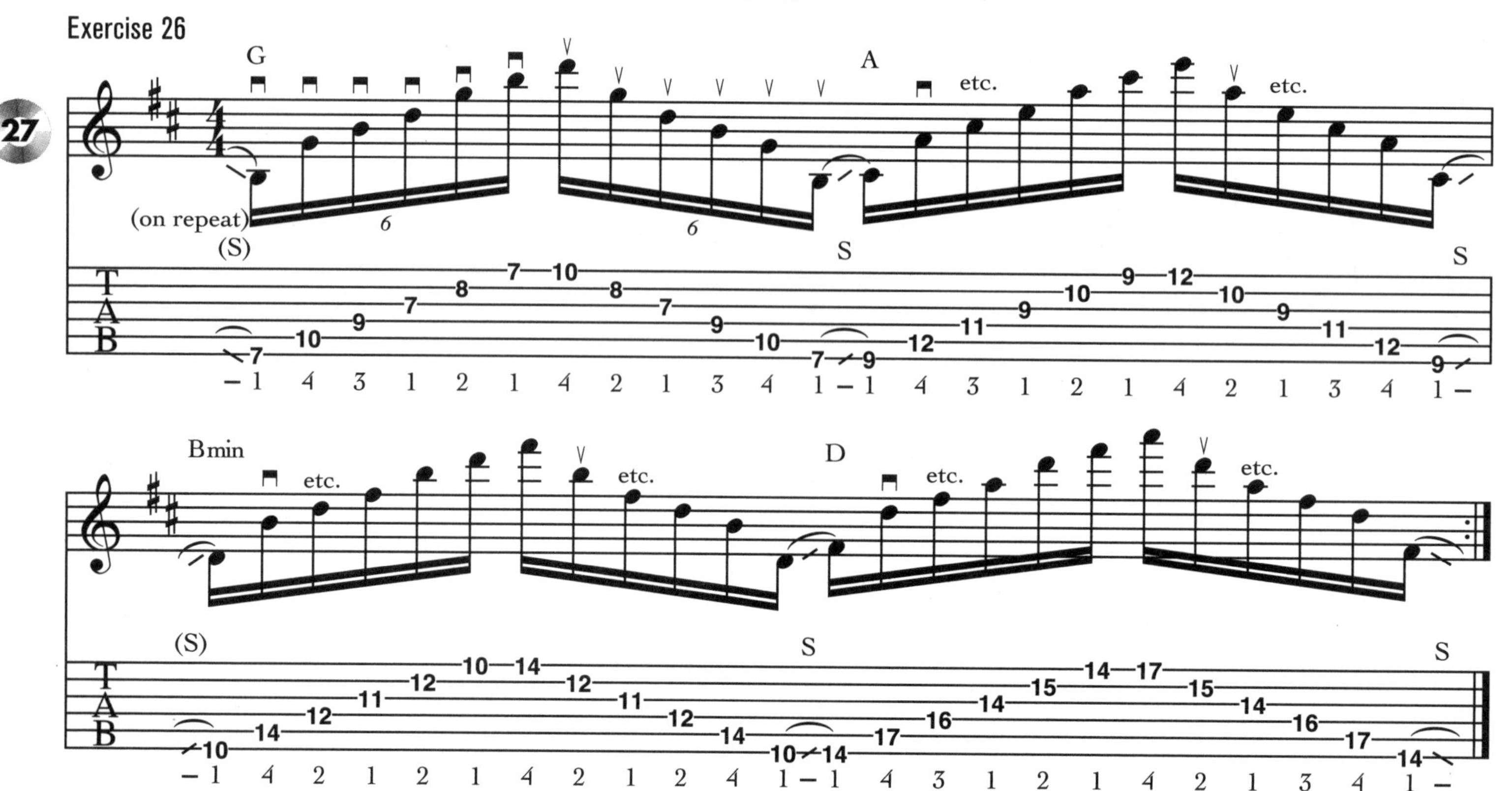

CHAPTER 6: MIXING SWEEP PICKING AND ALTERNATE PICKING

The exercises on the following pages represent a style of sweep picking that is both impressive and comparatively easy to play. It mixes in a few alternate-picked notes with sweeping. Each note is picked, and there are no hammer-ons or pull-offs. This style is "shape" oriented. The right-hand picking patterns are identical for most of the examples. The left hand changes only to accommodate the right-hand "shape." This tracking of the right-hand "shape" causes the addition of extensions such as 9ths and 7ths to the arpeggios. These extra notes make the arpeggios easier to play and cooler sounding at the same time. The first step will be to learn the right-hand picking "shape."

Exercise 27 shows the picking pattern starting on the 6th, 5th, and 4th strings. Mute the strings with your left-hand 1st finger. Learn the picking pattern by itself first. Notice how it is exactly the same, no matter which string you begin on.

Exercise 27A

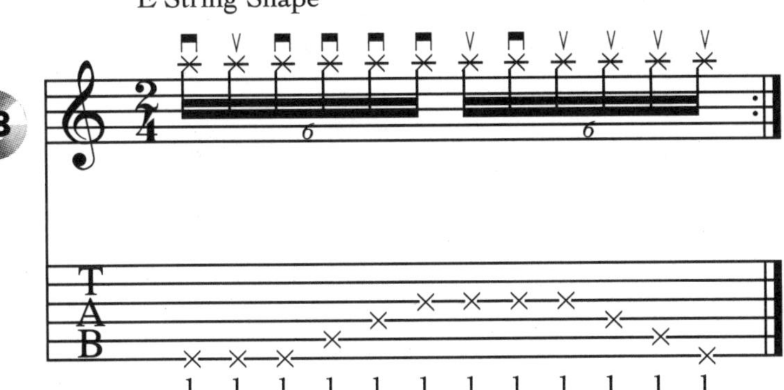

Exercise 27B

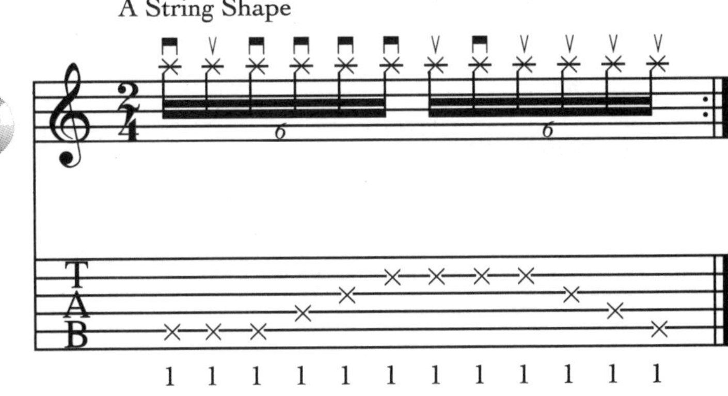

Exercise 27C

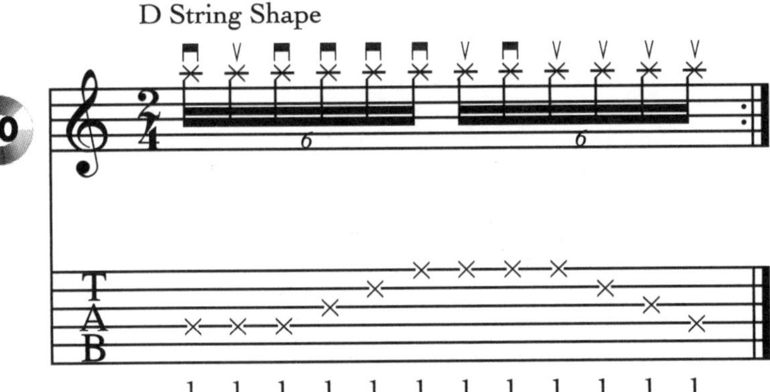

Now that you have learned the picking shape, use it to practice the movable arpeggio forms on pages 22 and 23, which are also rooted on the 6th, 5th, and 4th strings.

See the Human Sequencer Syndrome on page 64 for an example of these arpeggios in action.

Movable Arpeggio Forms

Exercise 28

C, Root on 6th String

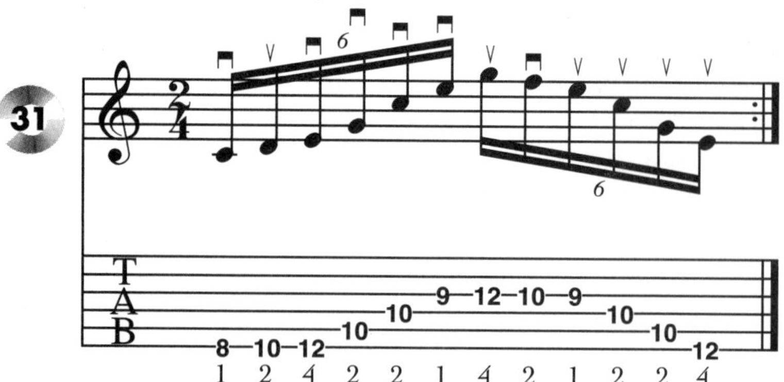

Exercise 29

Cmin, Root on 6th String

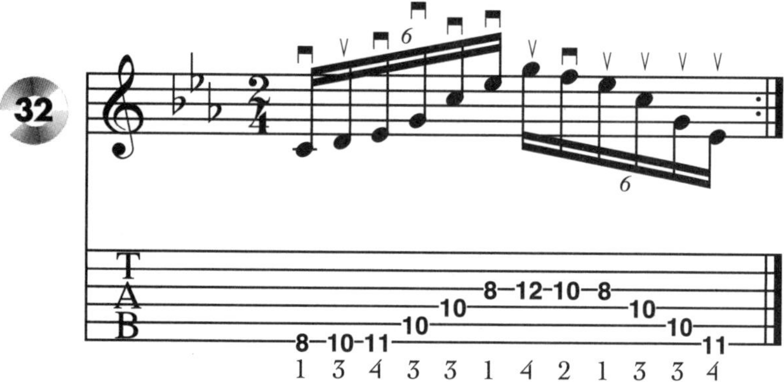

Exercise 30

Bmin7♭5, Root on 6th String

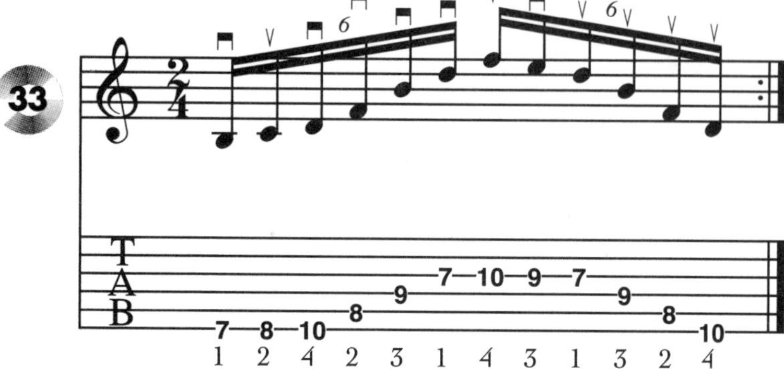

Exercise 31

F, Root on 5th String

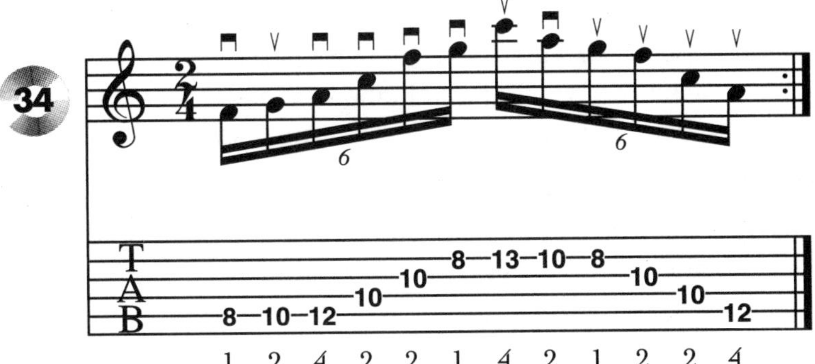

Exercise 32

Amin9, Root on 4th String

Exercise 33

AMaj7, Root on 4th String

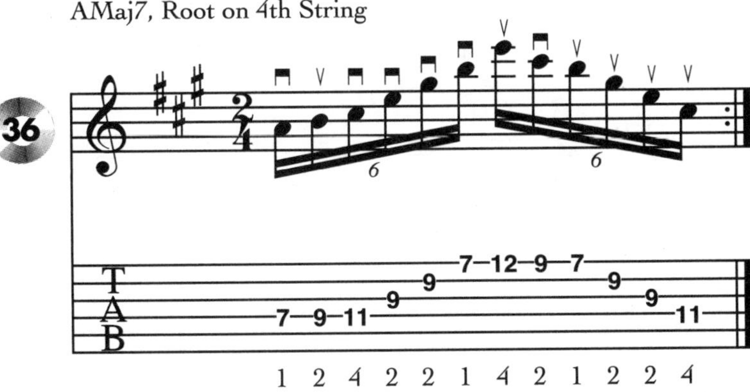

CHAPTER 7: TREMOLO PICKING

Tremolo picking, which is often called "trem picking" for short, is the rapid and continuous picking of a note or notes. This exciting melodic technique is commonly used in rock music. Surf guitar master Dick Dale used it to play melody of his legendary surf standard "Miserlou." Eddie Van Halen used it in "Hot for Teacher," "Eruption," and many other songs, and Stevie Ray Vaughan used it on "Dirty Pool" and others. Trem picking is simply fast alternate picking on a single string or set of adjacent strings. It can be achieved by picking from the whole arm or from the wrist. You may hear it in blues, rock, Spanish (classical), and many other styles of guitar music. The exercises below will give you a good start on trem picking.

To get started, try Exercise 34, which is merely picking rapidly and continuously on the open 6th string. Next, try trem picking the two-octave C Major scale form that follows.

Exercise 34

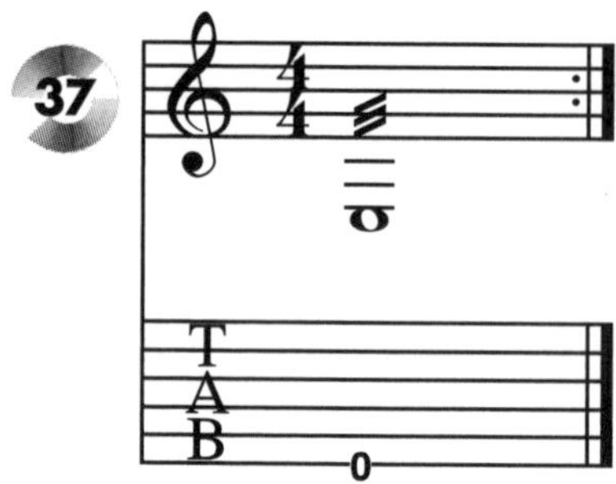

Exercise 35

This exercise is in the style of Eddie Van Halen. It is an A Minor scale moving up the 3rd string and culminating in a bend to E, the 5th of the key.

Exercise 36

This one is in the style of Dick Dale. Note the accents ⟩ on the sixteenth notes. Stressing these notes by playing them louder is essential.

Exercise 37

Exercise 38 presents trem picking *double stops* (two notes played at once). In this case, the double stops are diatonic 3rds in E Minor. (The term *diatonic* means belonging to the key.)

Exercise 38

CHAPTER 8: PENTATONIC RIFFS AND CONCEPTS

The Minor Pentatonic Scale

The *minor pentatonic scale* is arguably the most common and easy scale found in rock lead guitar. It has only five notes, as you may have guessed from the Greek word *penta*, which means five. The formula of the scale is as follows: three half steps, whole step, whole step, three half steps, whole step. See the scale index on page 72 for five minor pentatonic scale forms.

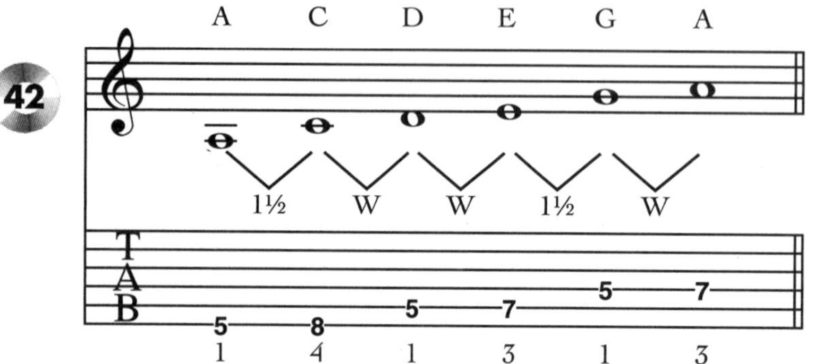

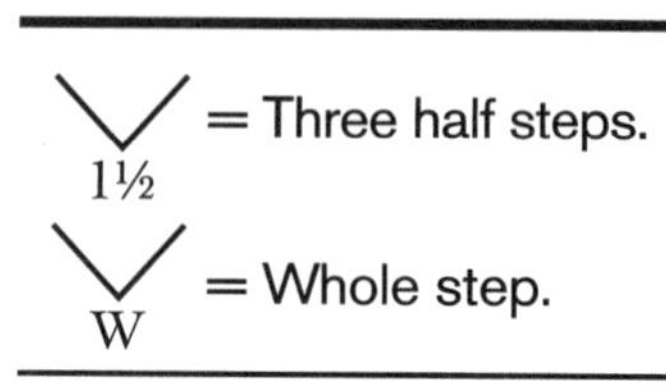

The Blues Scale

The most common variation on this scale is the *blues scale*. Even though it is called a blues scale, it is used in many forms of music, including rock. Its formula is: three half steps, whole step, half step, half step, three half steps, whole step. This scale has six tones instead of five. The added tone is a passing tone between the 4th and 5th degrees of the minor pentatonic scale called the ♭5. See the scale index on page 76 for five blues scale forms.

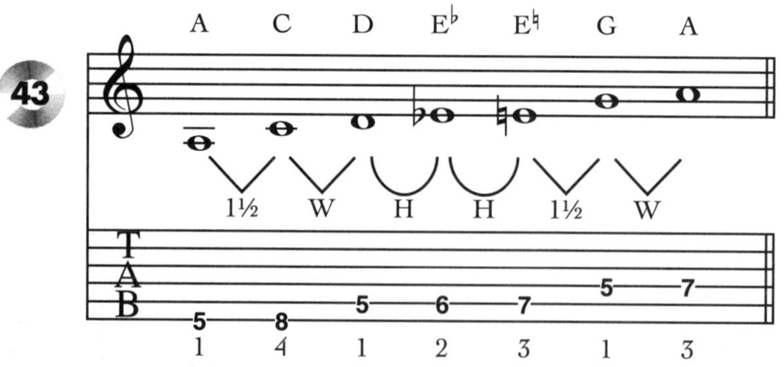

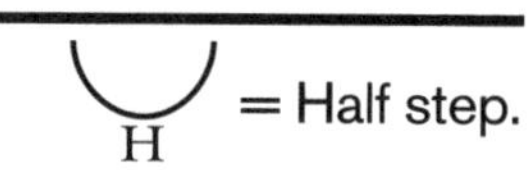

Try out this exercise. It includes an easy *position-shifting* (moving from one position to another) technique. As you are about to learn, it will lead to some interesting possibilities.

Exercise 39

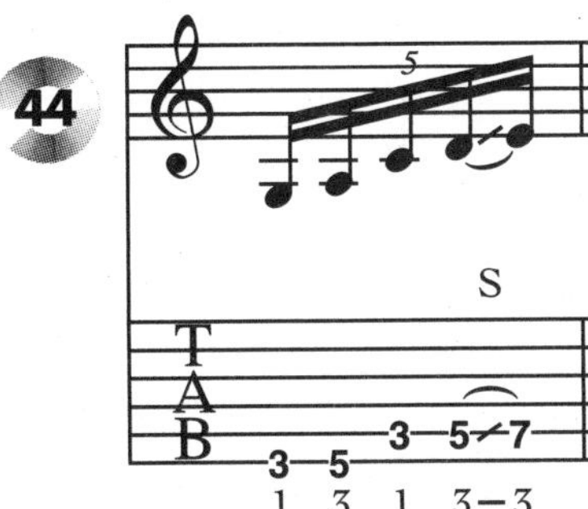

Here, the same technique is used three times in a row, starting on different strings each time. This is a fun and easy way to move around in the A Minor Pentatonic scale.

Exercise 40

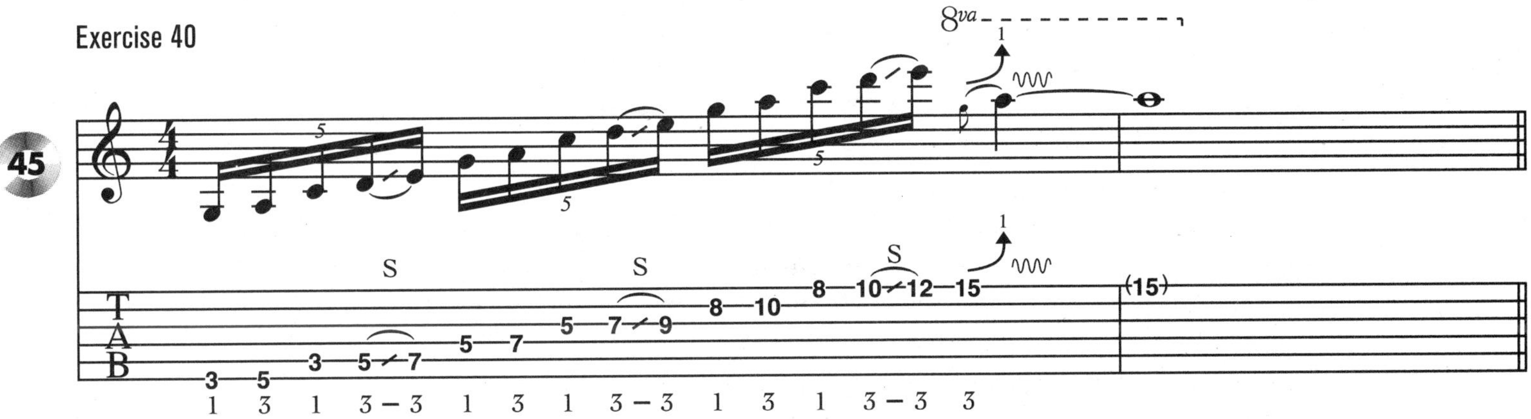

Try this typical rock riff, which uses the same position-shifting technique. It also uses the A Minor Pentatonic scale.

Exercise 41

Below, you'll find 16 versatile and useful pentatonic/blues riffs. Learn to repeat each riff and groove on it—the faster, the better. Then, practice playing one riff four times then skipping to another for four times, etc. You should also try improvising pentatonic scale passages, then settling into one of the riffs for a while. Each riff is numbered, and there is an explanation of each riff. Each riff is movable so it can be used in any key.

This bluesy, rockin' riff is easy to play and can be used over E Minor, E Major, or E7.

Riff #1

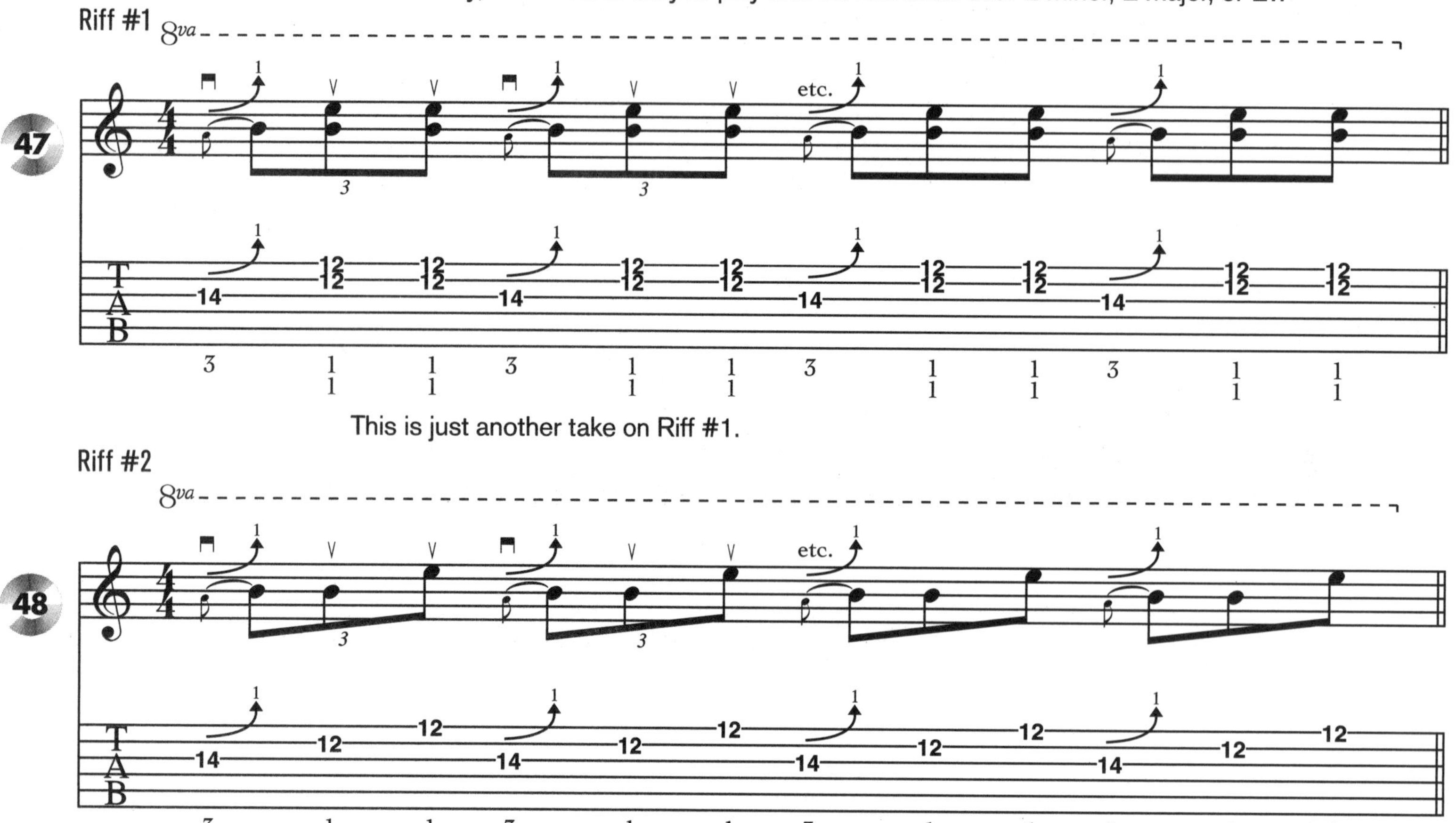

This is just another take on Riff #1.

Riff #2

Check out this rock blues riff in E. It is used by many players.

Riff #3

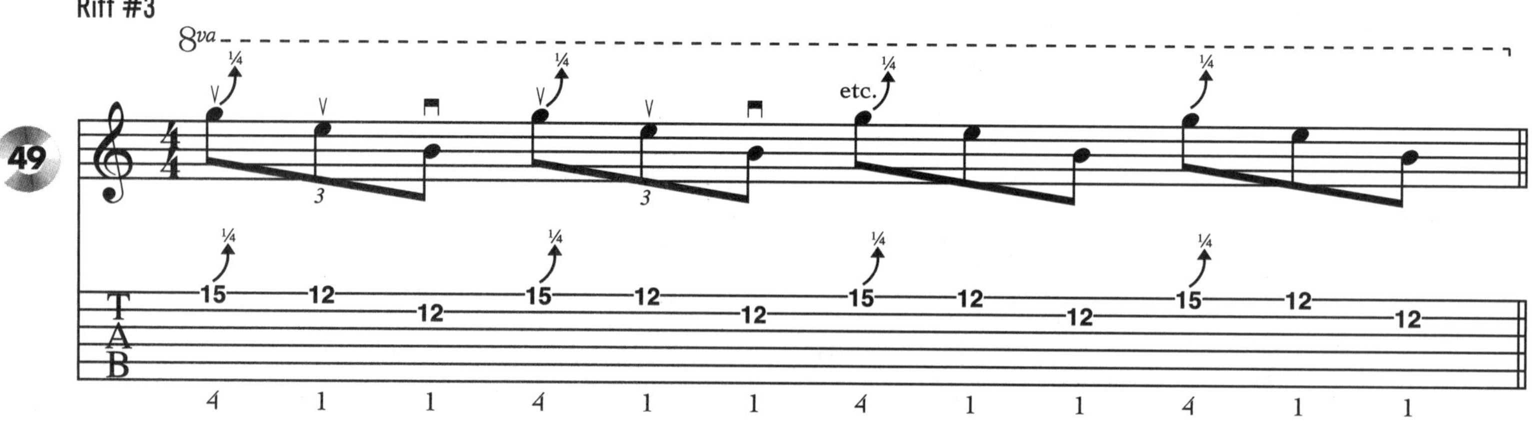

Riff #4 is also easy and works best over E Minor or E 7.

Riff #4

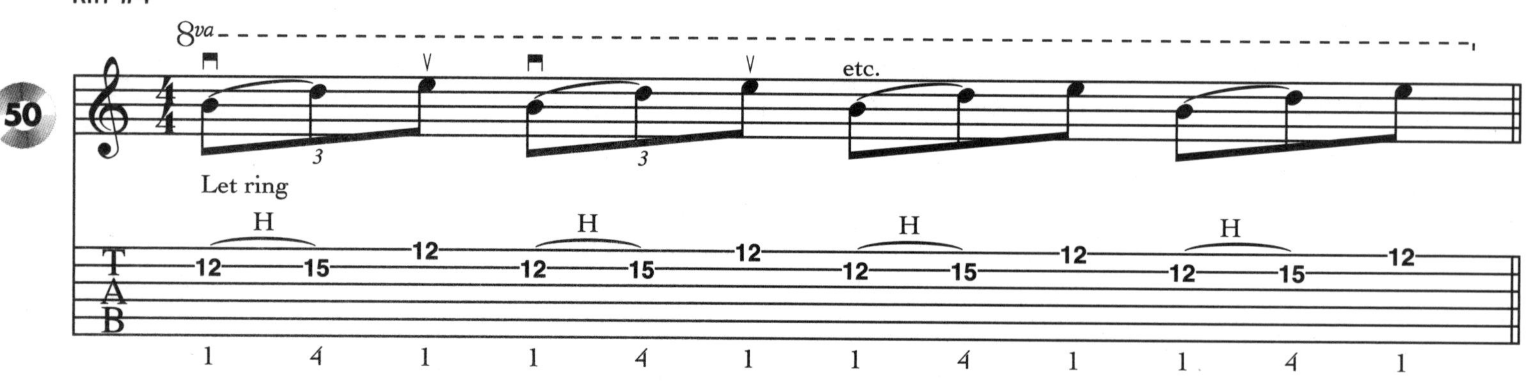

This one is in the style of Jimmy Page and works best over E Minor or G.

Riff #5

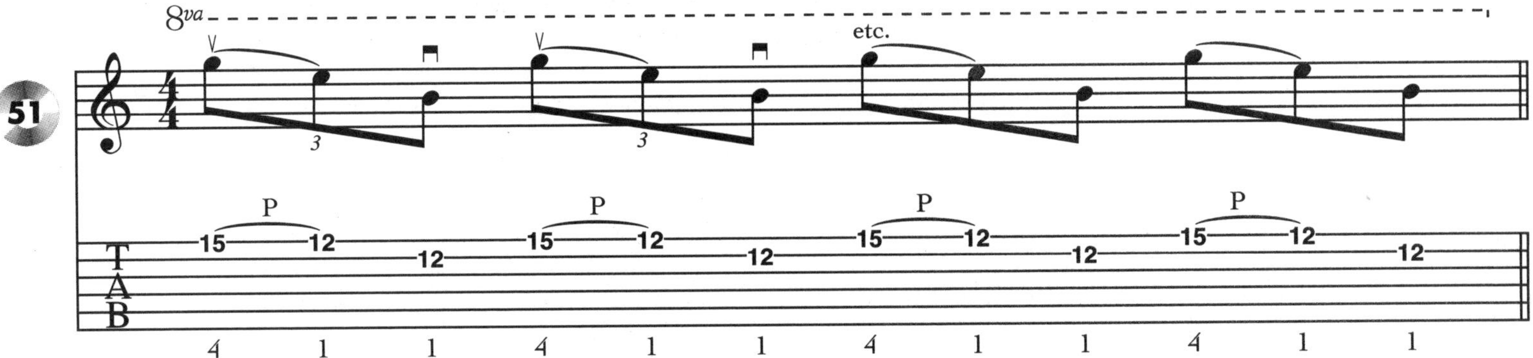

Riff #6 is probably the biggest rock 'n' roll lead riff of all time. Try it over E Minor, G, or E7.

Riff #6

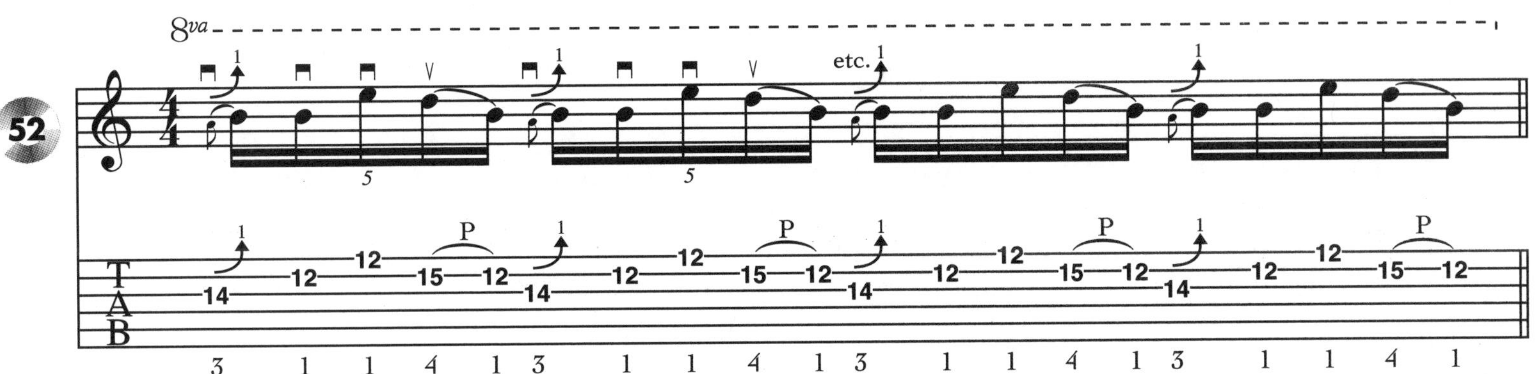

This is another take on Riff #6.

Riff #7

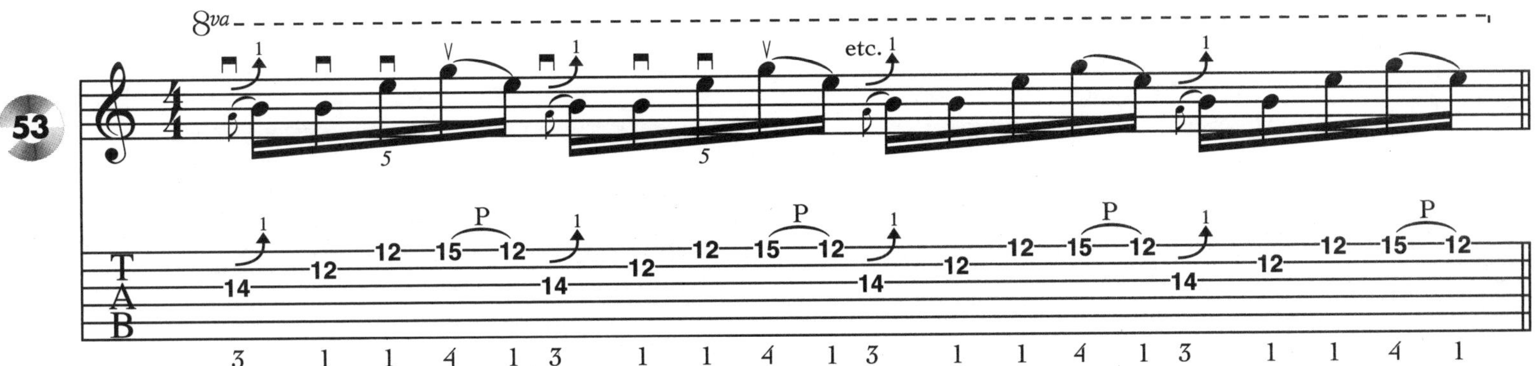

This one combines Riffs #6 and #7.

Riff #8

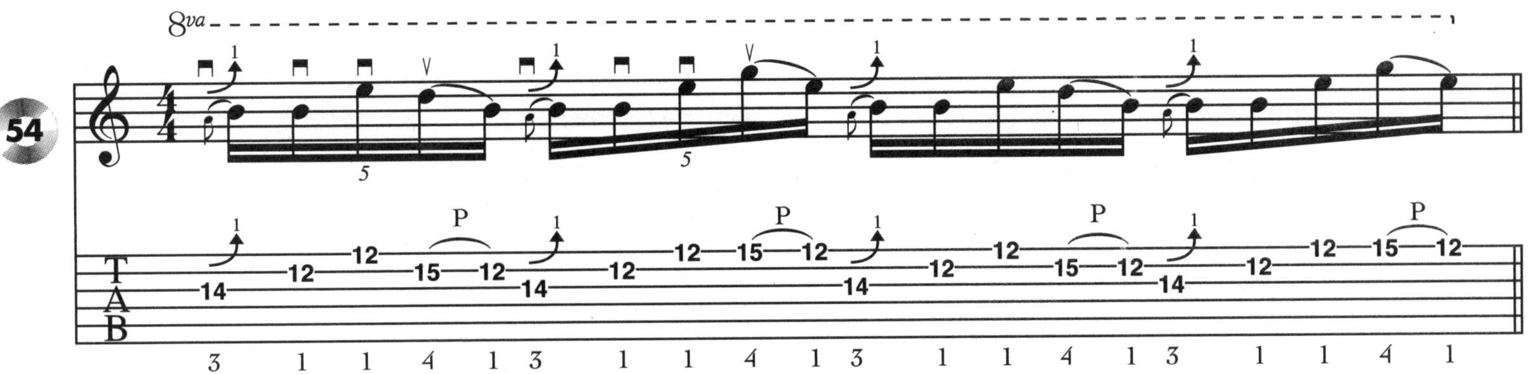

Here's another one in the style of Jimmy Page. It works well in E Minor or G.

Riff #9

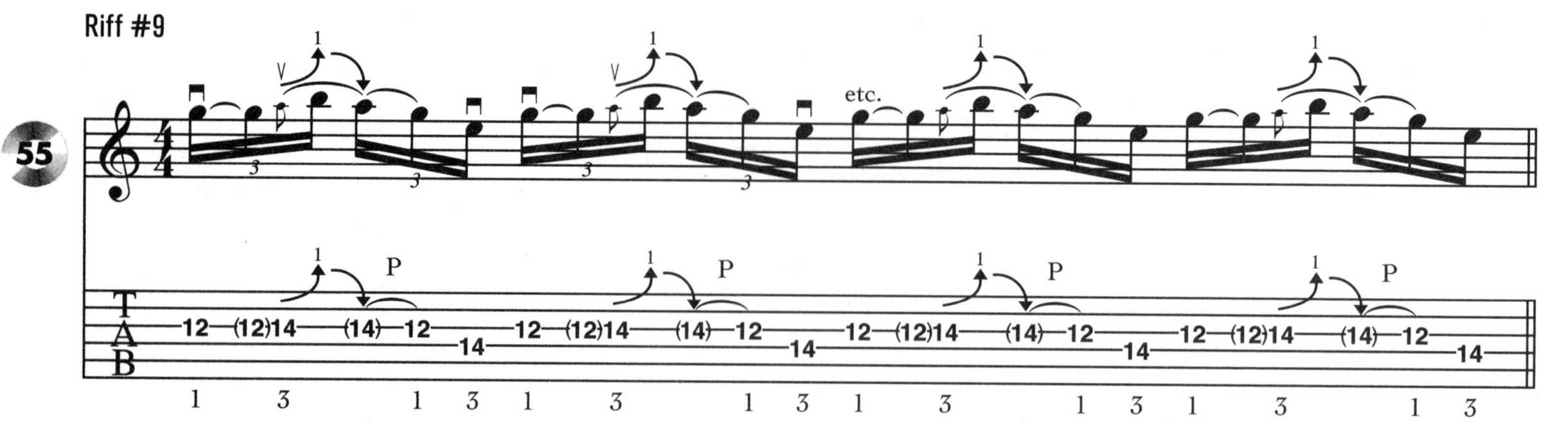

This riff is in the style of Ace Frehley. It incorporates the ♭5 and works well over E Minor, E7, or G.

Riff #10

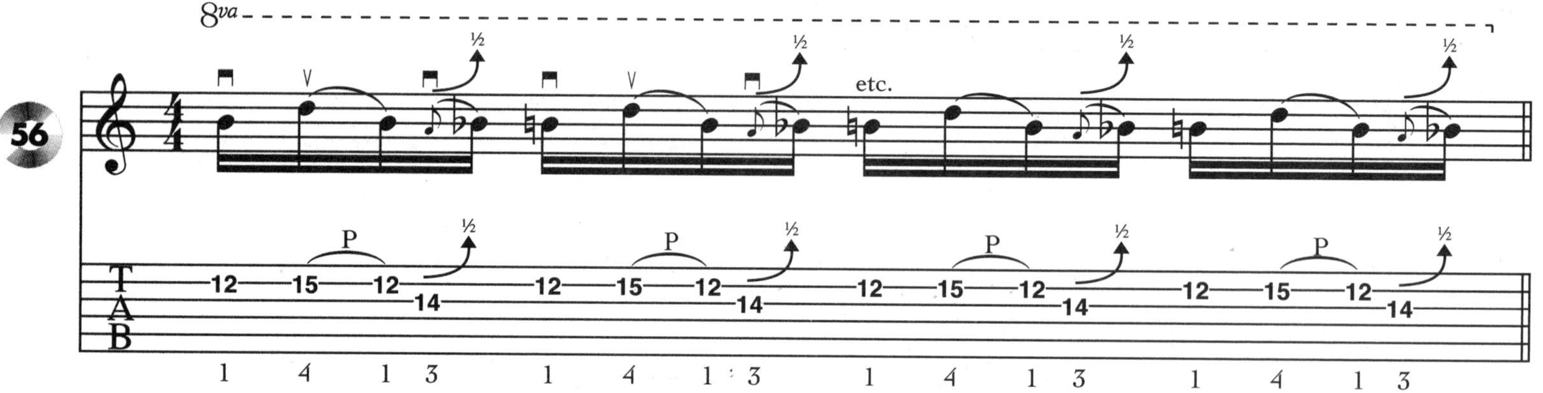

This is another take on Riff #10.

Riff #11

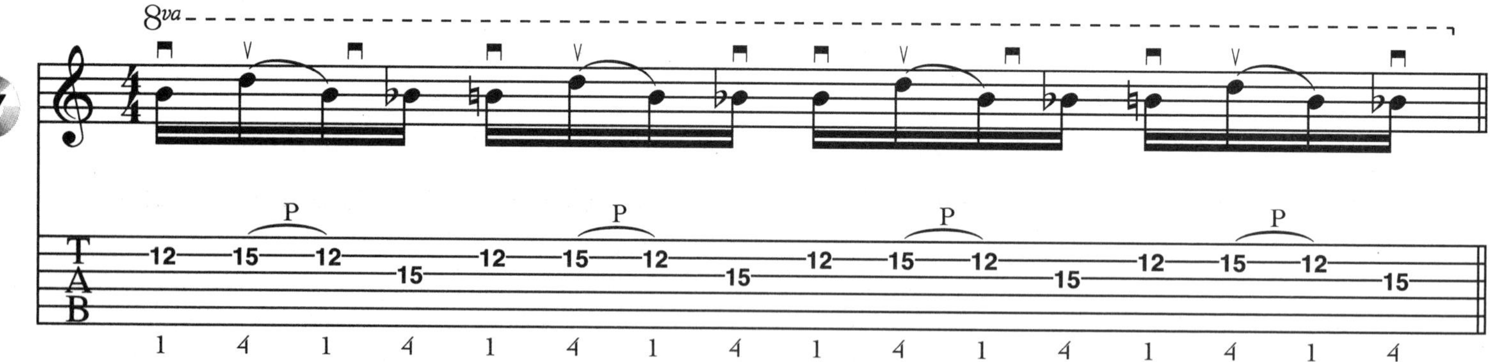

This riff combines Riffs #10 and #11.

Riff #12

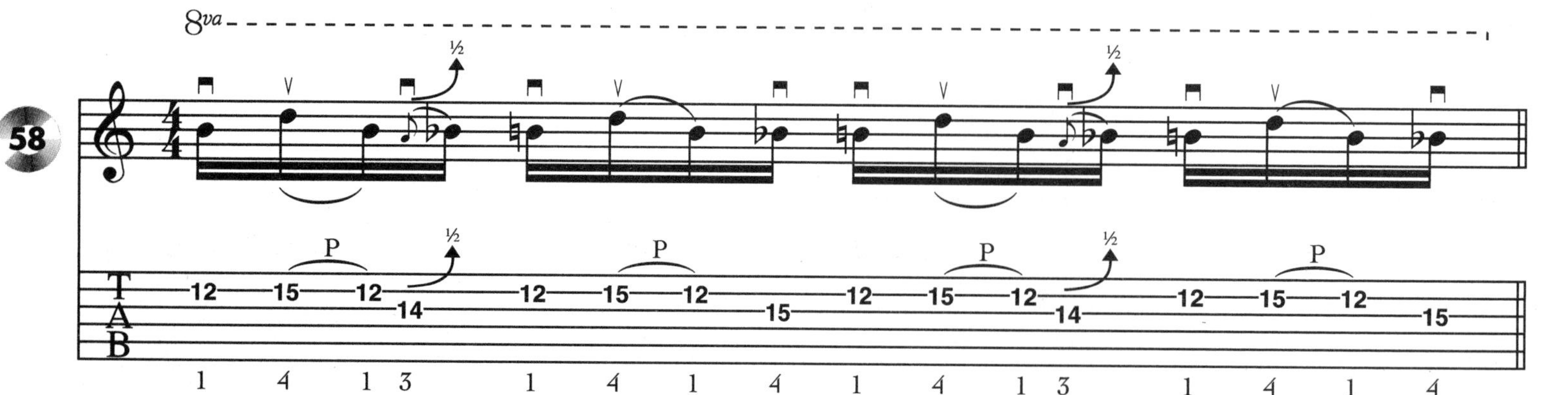

This riff is in the style of Eddie Hazel (Funkadelic guitarist) and works well over E Minor or G.

Riff #13

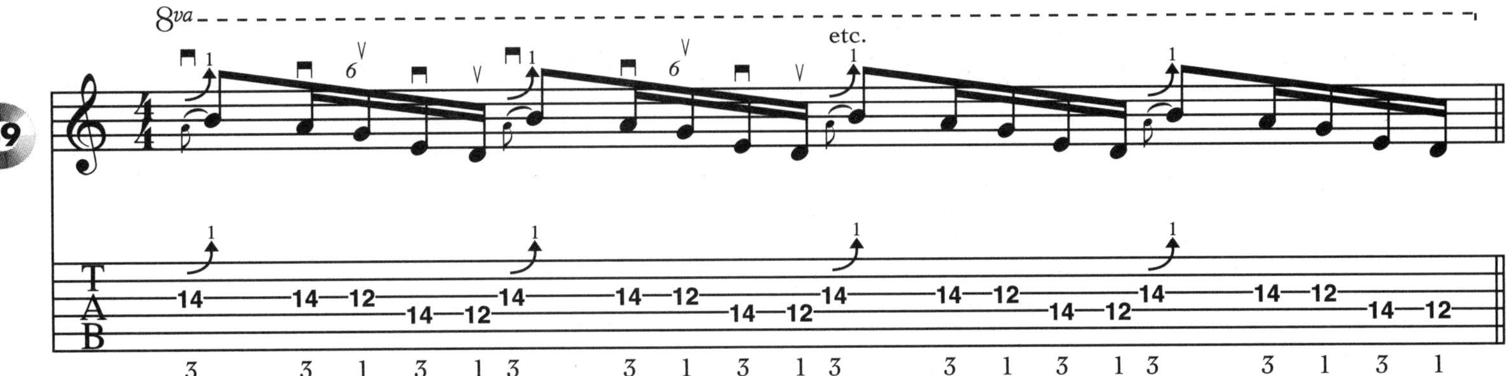

This Southern-rock style riff incorporates the ♭5 and works well over E Minor or G.

Riff #14

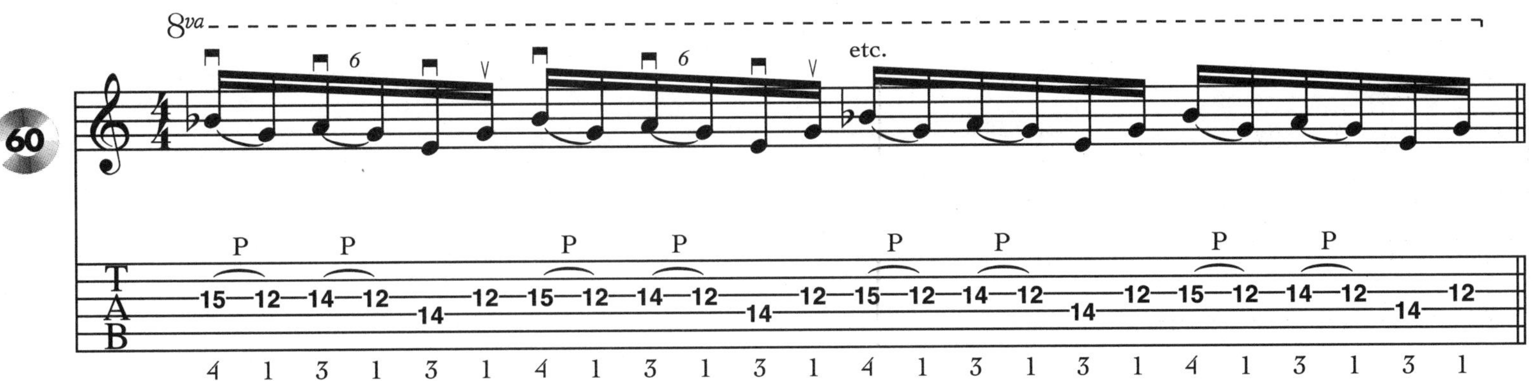

In the style of Jimi Hendrix, this riff works well over E Minor or G.

Riff #15

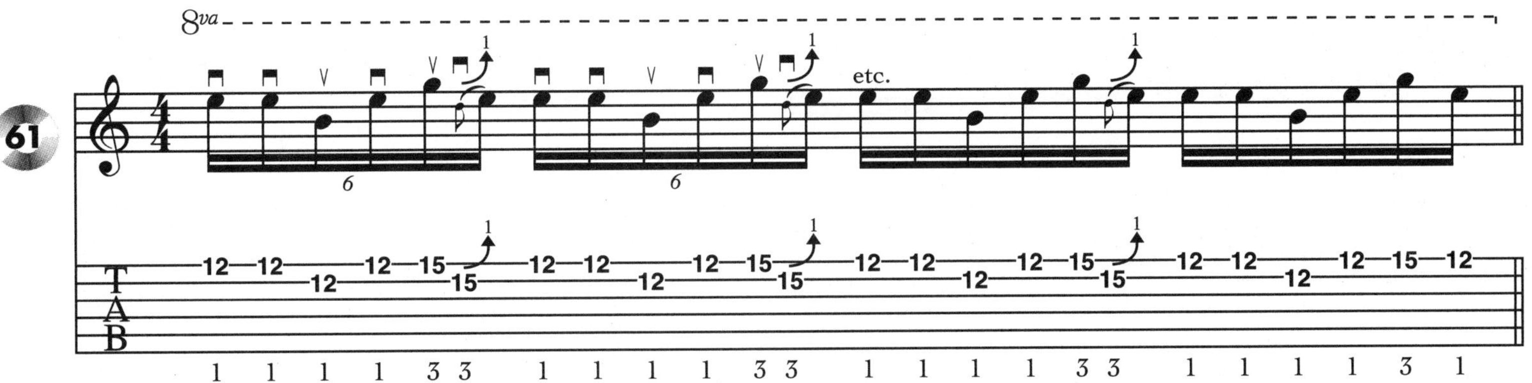

This riff is also in the style of Jimi Hendrix and works well over E Minor or E7.

Riff #16

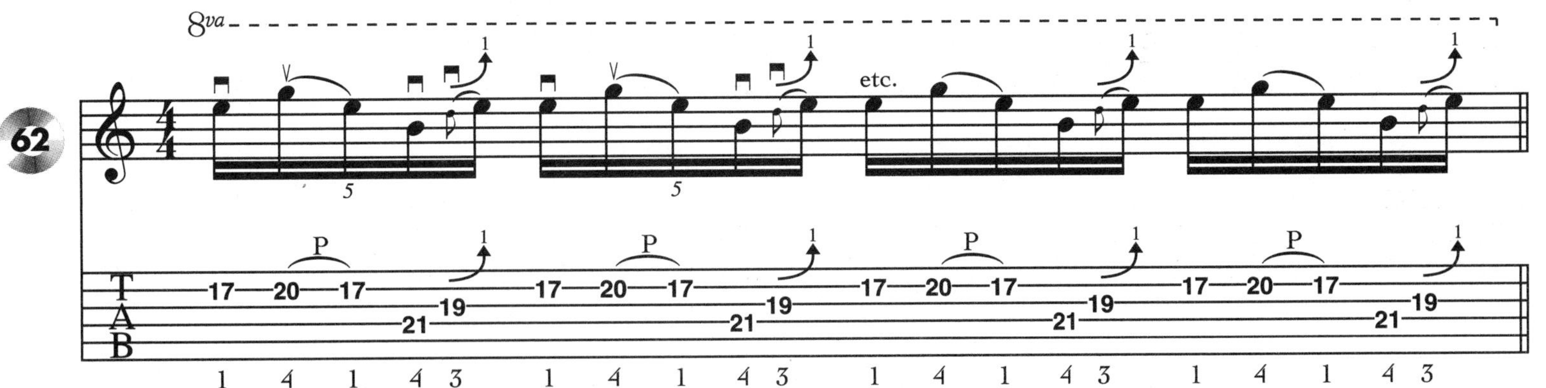

Combining Minor Pentatonic Scales

So far, the pentatonic concepts we've covered have been very basic. Now, let's get into something deeper. Three minor pentatonic scales can fit into the same major key. Here's how it works: Minor pentatonic scales, modes, or chords can be built on the 2nd, 3rd, and 6th degrees of any major scale. The notes in C Major are: C–D–E–F–G–A–B–C. The 2nd, 3rd, and 6th scale tones are D, E, and A. So, the D, E, and A Minor Pentatonic scales contain notes exclusively from C Major.

> D Minor Pentatonic = D–F–G–A–C
> E Minor Pentatonic = E–G–A–B–D
> A Minor Pentatonic = A–C–D–E–G

By combining all of the scale tones from these three scales, all of the notes in C Major can be found. This leads to many interesting riffs, one of which is shown below.

Exercise 42

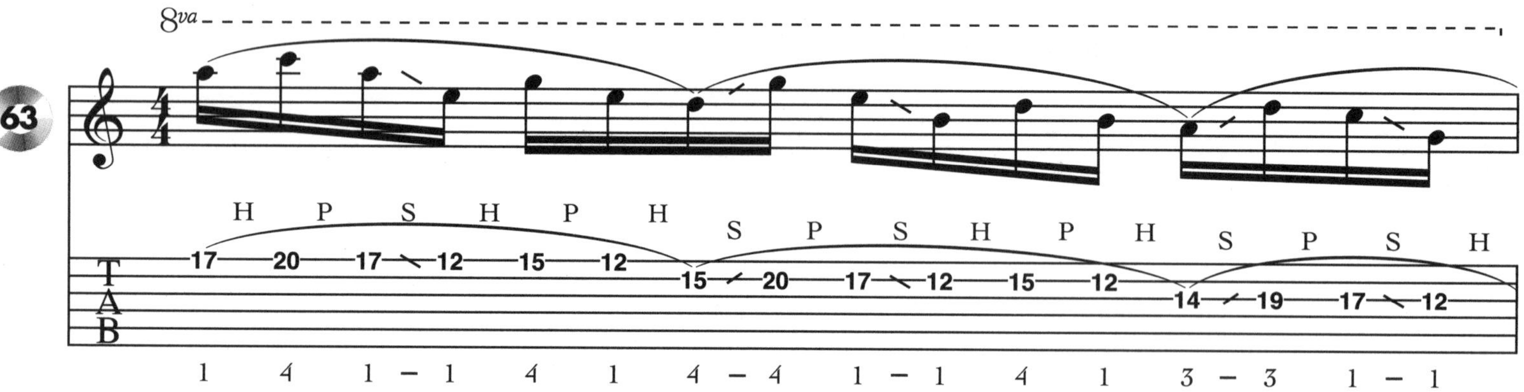

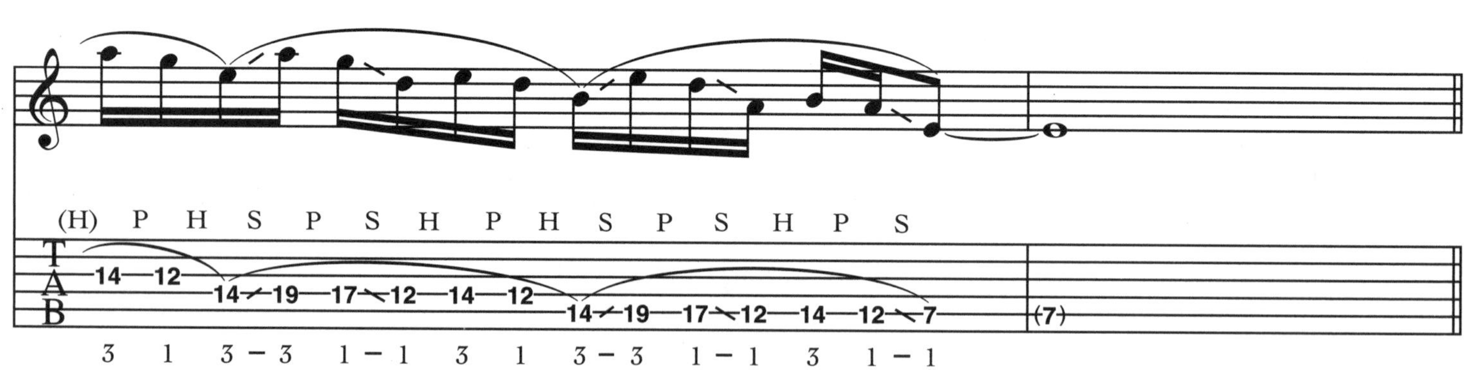

CHAPTER 9: SCALE SEQUENCING

Scale sequencing (repeating a melodic shape on different pitches) is a powerful and common tool in virtually any form of music, from Mozart to Metallica. Rock 'n' roll lead guitar is chock-full of it. To hear some excellent examples of scale sequencing in action, listen to Randy Rhoads's screaming solo on Ozzy Osbourne's "Flying High Again," and Kirk Hammett's classic work on Metallica's "Seek and Destroy." Sequencing is the art of organizing the tones of any scale into a logical and repeating pattern that ascends and descends through the scale. It is most easily thought of by assigning numbers to the tones of the scale.

C	D	E	F	G	A	B	C
1	2	3	4	5	6	7	8 (1)

Once the numbers are assigned, they are grouped into patterns, like so: 1–2–3, 2–3–4, 3–4–5, 4–5–6, etc; or 1–2–3–4, 2–3–4–5, 3–4–5–6, 4–5–6–7, etc.; or 1–3, 2–4, 3–6, 4–7, etc. Melodic sequences result from playing the scales in this way. The possibilities are nearly endless.

Here are some popular sequences, all of which are played in a one-octave A Natural Minor scale.

Exercise 43—"Threes" Sequence

Exercise 44—"Fours" Sequence

Exercise 45—Diatonic 3rds Sequence

This slippery, legato "threes" sequence is longer, incorporates pull-offs, and uses the E Blues scale.

Exercise 46

Here is a scorching riff that repeats adjacent groups of a "threes" sequence in the E Blues scale. Enjoy!

Exercise 47

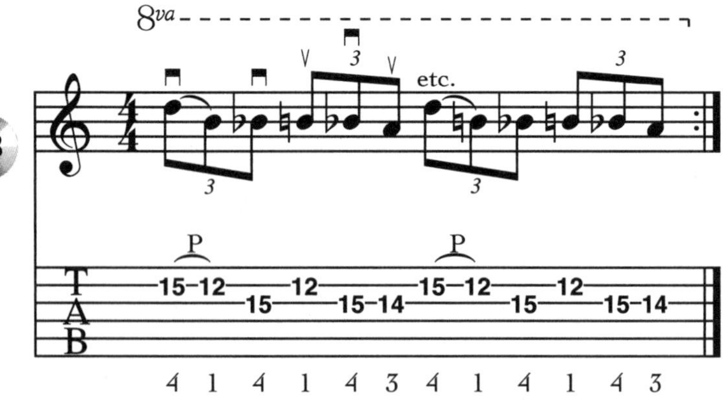

Many other pages in this book also feature scale sequences. A few examples are Exercise 5 on page 12, Exercise 6 on page 13, and Exercise 10 on page 15, to name a few.

CHAPTER 10: SINGLE-STRING CONCEPTS

Getting around on one string is a very important lead guitar skill. It helps with position shifting and also promotes more musical phrasing. There are countless ways of playing hot riffs and licks on one string. The five examples that follow use the natural notes on the 3rd string, so these examples can be used in C Major, A Minor, or any related mode. You should "run with the ball" and learn these concepts on other strings and in other keys.

Exercise 48 introduces the natural notes on the 3rd string. Its purpose is simply to familiarize you with playing the natural notes on a single string, which will help prepare you for the examples that follow. You should also learn to play the natural notes on all of the other strings.

Exercise 48

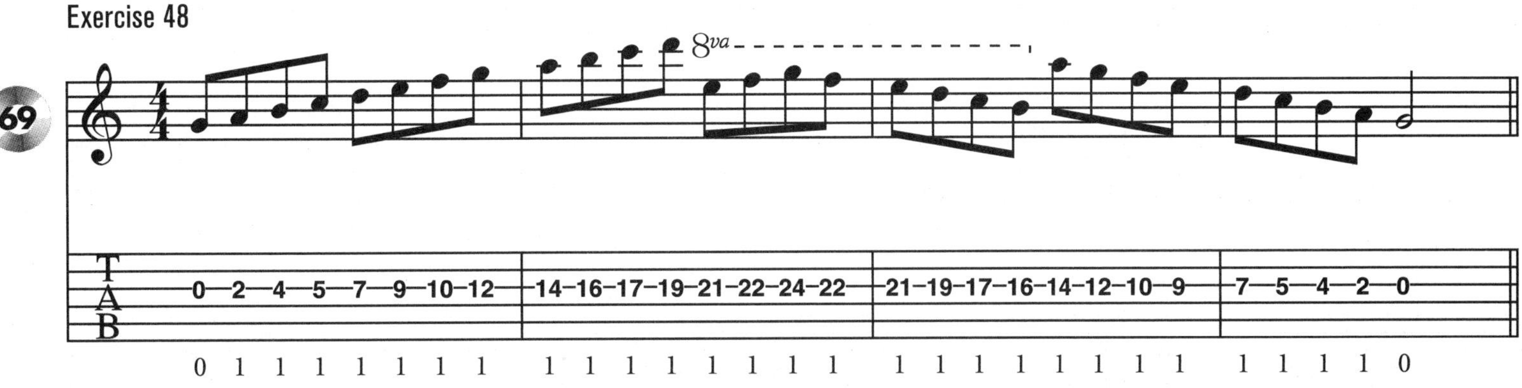

This example shows how to slide to adjacent scale tones on the 3rd string.

Exercise 49

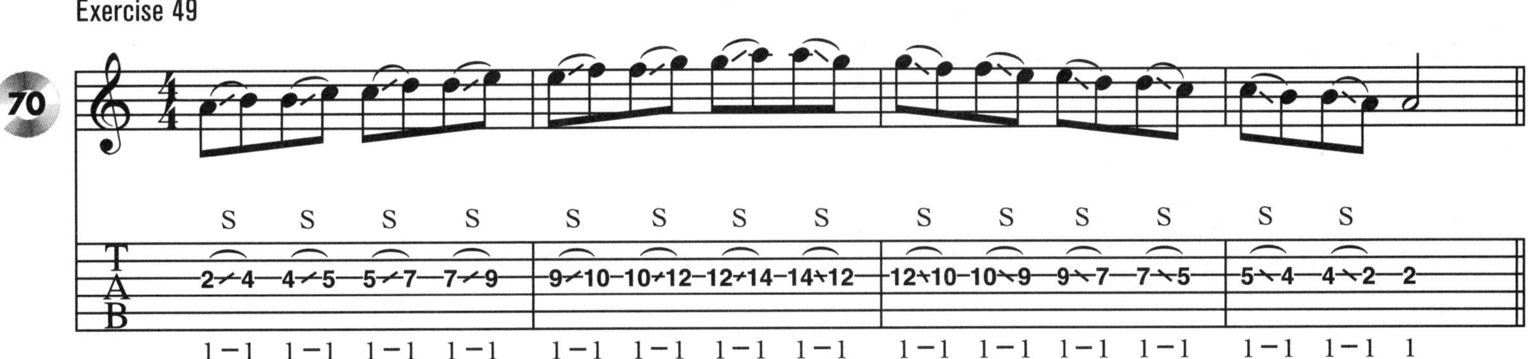

This example expands on the previous concept. It shows how to slide to non-adjacent scale tones on the 3rd string.

Exercise 50

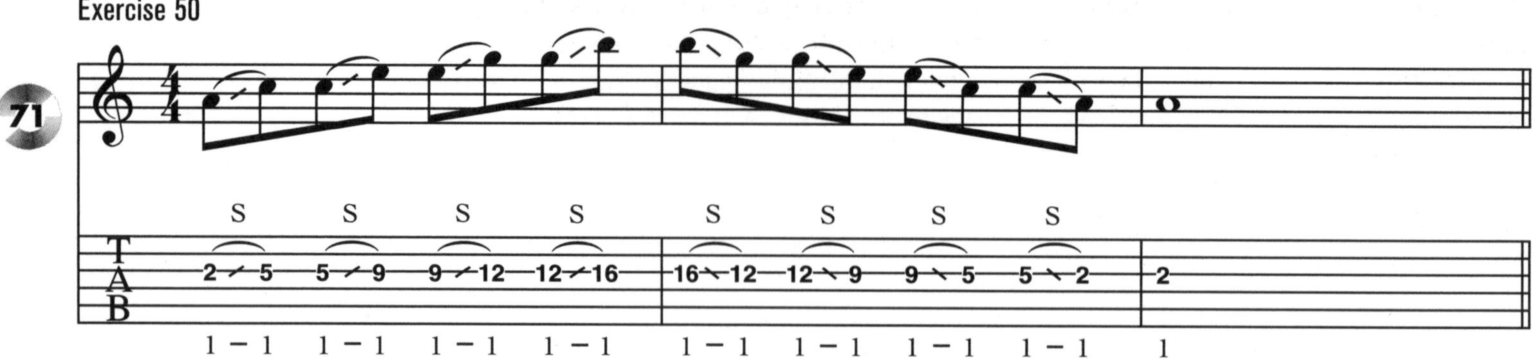

This example shows how to do a rapid-fire alternate-picked sequence on the 3rd string.

Exercise 51

This example expands on the previous concept by "sequencing the sequence."

Exercise 52

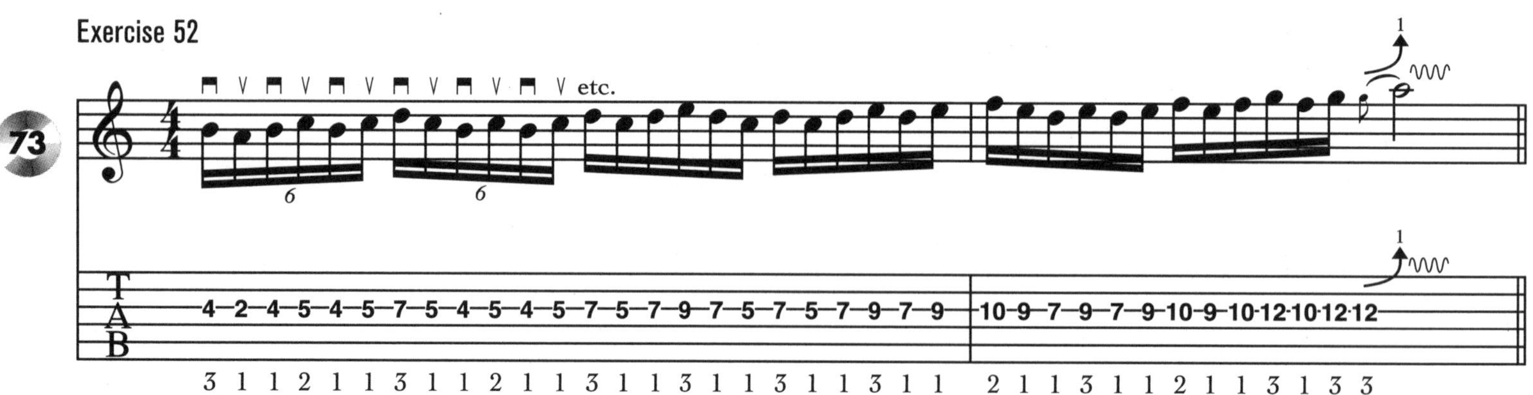

CHAPTER 11: DOUBLE STOPS

On a stringed instrument, a double stop consists of stopping, or playing, two strings at once. Double stops, also called *dyads*, are often chord fragments or notes from the same scale. Double stops are used in all kinds of music, especially blues and rock lead guitar. The diagrams below will illustrate how a symmetrical series of double stops can be created using notes from the major scale.

Exercise 53

G Major Scale, Form #5 (D Form)

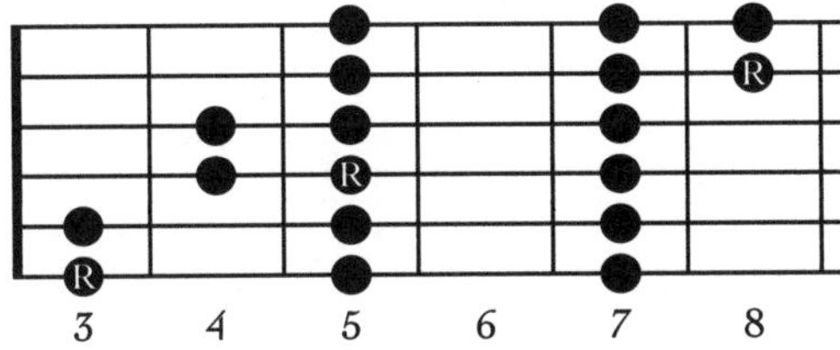

Extract Two Straight Lines of Notes from the Scale Form

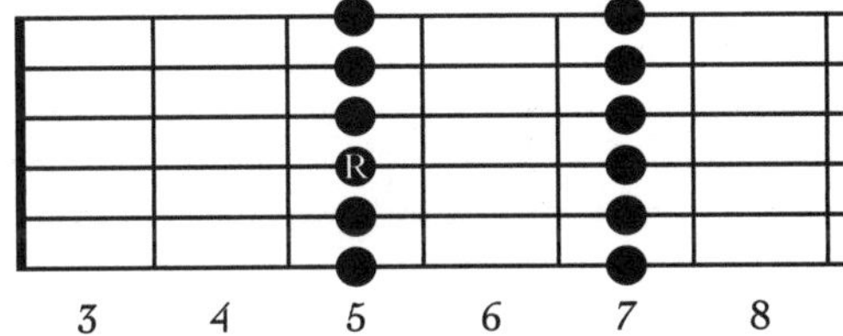

Exercise 54 shows a "double stop scale," created from the notes in the second diagram above. All of these notes are in the key of A Dorian (see page 77). Soloing with these double stops is very effective over any blues progression in A or over a Dorian vamp in A, such as Amin–D9.

Exercise 54

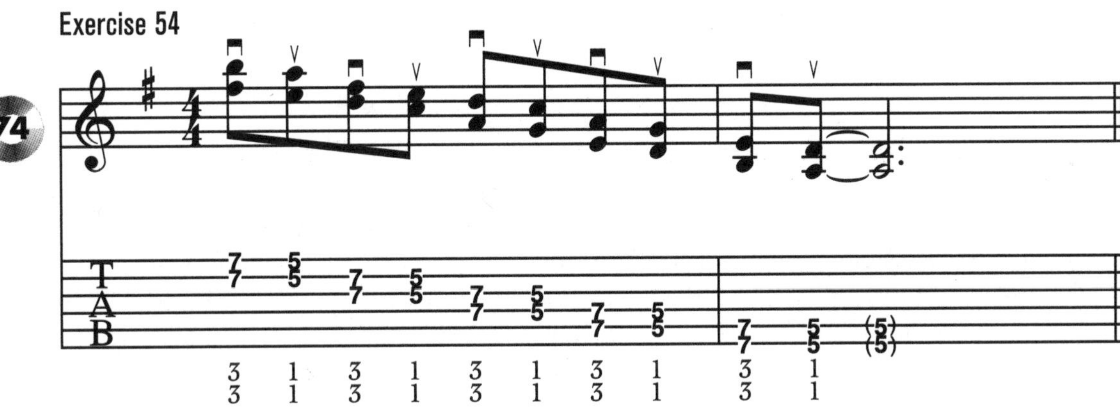

This bluesy exercise weaves a few double stops into an A Minor Pentatonic riff. Try it at your next blues jam!

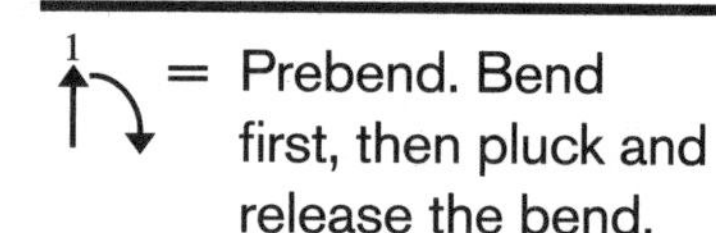

Exercise 55

This swingin' blues phrase incorporates open strings and is in the style of Stevie Ray Vaughan.

Exercise 56

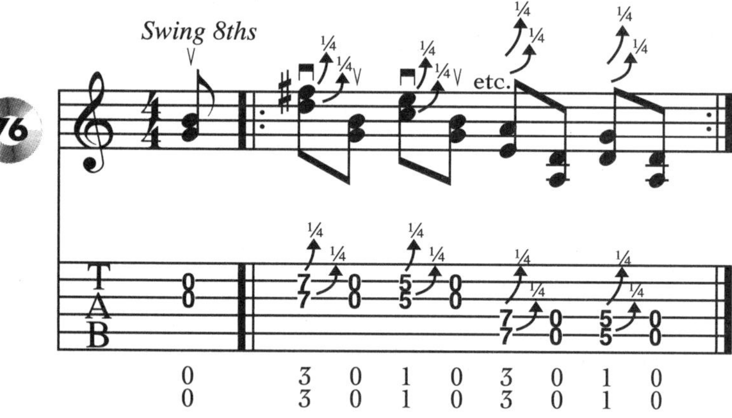

This diagram shows the C Major scale over the entire fretboard. The roots are not indicated. Instead, a series of double stops on the 1st and 2nd strings are circled. These intervals are perfect 4ths, so all you have to do is barre the two high strings to play them. Sliding these double stops around makes position shifting easy and also leads to some very cool phrasing ideas.

Exercise 57

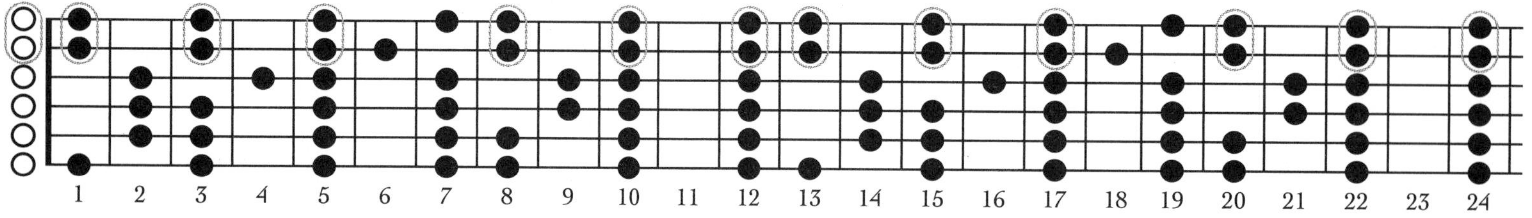

This exercise shows how to ascend and descend through the perfect 4ths in the key of C Major.
This will also work while jamming in A Minor.

Exercise 58

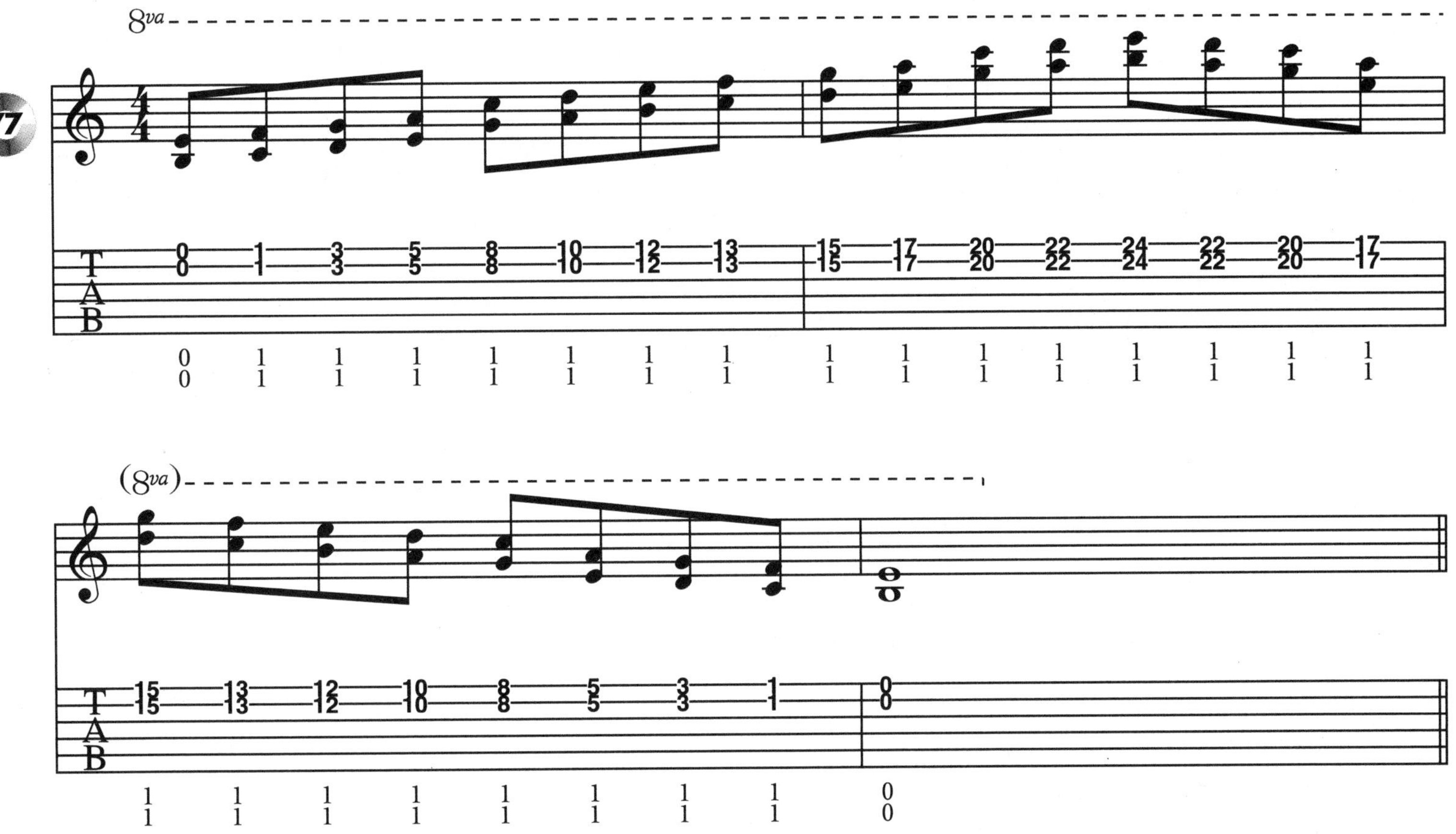

Exercise 59 shows one of many ways that the double stops from Exercise 58 can be woven into
a musical phrase.

Exercise 59

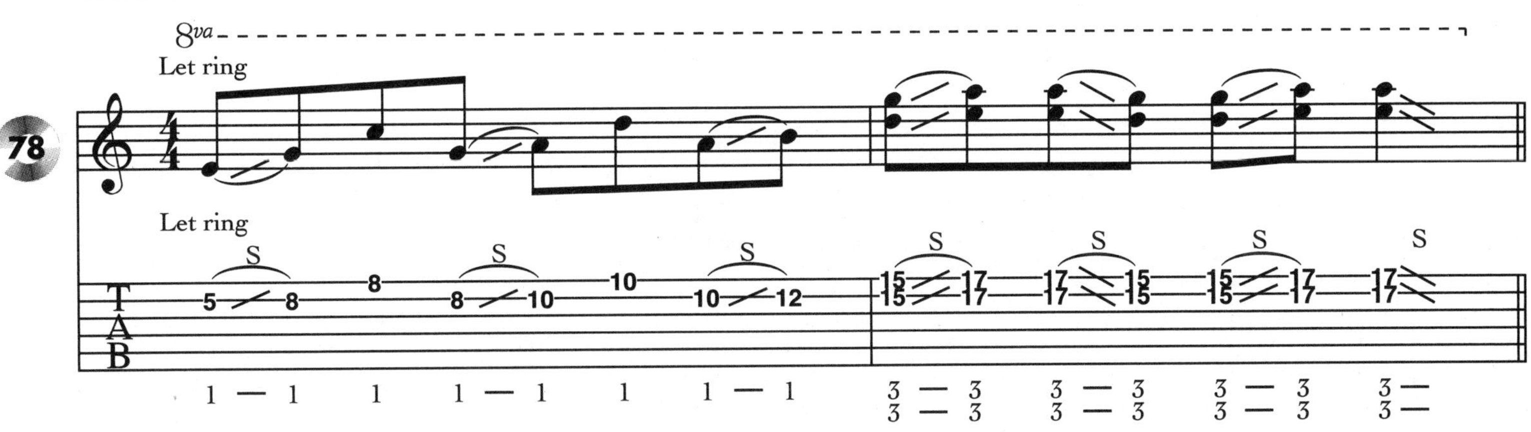

CHAPTER 12: HARMONIZED LEADS

Both live and in the studio, the sweet, sustaining sound of two electric guitars in harmony is often the perfect touch. Kiss's "Detroit Rock City," Bad Company's *"Can't Get Enough,"* and Joe Satriani's "Crushing Day" are all fine examples of this. In this chapter, we will go over several easy ways of harmonizing a lead riff. Knowledge of theory will be helpful in understanding this section. This is because good harmonization is achieved through a combination of using the ear and choosing the correct notes.

The easiest way to harmonize any diatonic phrase is to play the same phrase a diatonic 3rd higher.

Let's define some terms. As mentioned on page 25, diatonic means "belonging to the scale or key." A diatonic 3rd is an interval that separates two notes by a distance of three scale tones. Sometimes this distance is a major 3rd (two whole steps) and sometimes it is a minor 3rd (one-and-a-half steps). The diagram below should make this concept clear.

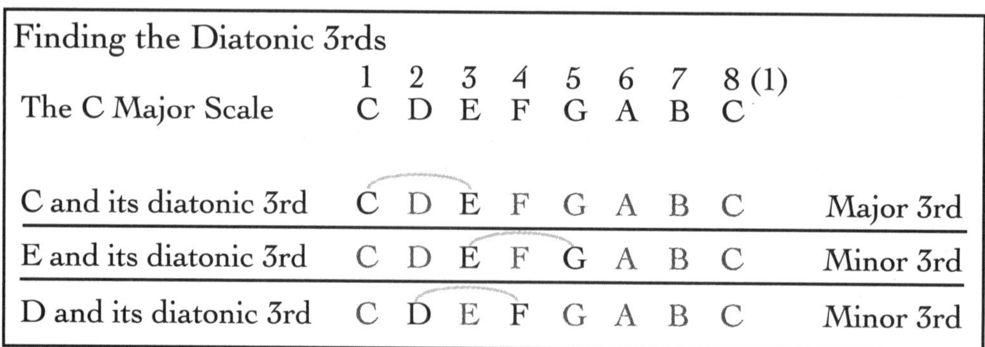

This example shows the C Major scale harmonized in diatonic 3rds. The small notes are the harmony.

Exercise 60

This example is a harmonized riff from the C Major scale.

Exercise 61

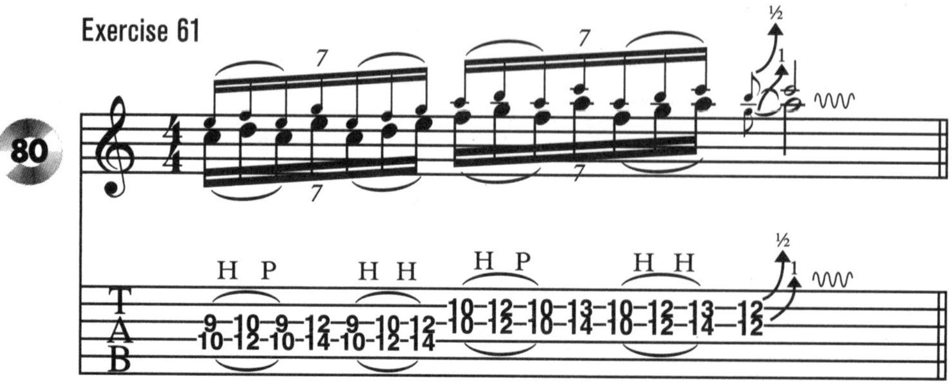

Note: If you want to hear this effect played on two guitars but do not have another guitarist to jam with, you can use an effects processor that features the "smart" harmony function to recreate the effect.

To harmonize a pentatonic or blues riff, play the same phrase in *parallel 5ths*. A parallel 5th is a phrase that is played with every note harmonized by a perfect 5th (a distance of three-and-a-half-steps higher). Most rock players are familiar with the *power chord*. This type of chord contains only a root and perfect 5th (see diagrams below).

This chord contains the root note E and its perfect 5th, B.

This chord contains the root note D and its perfect 5th, A.

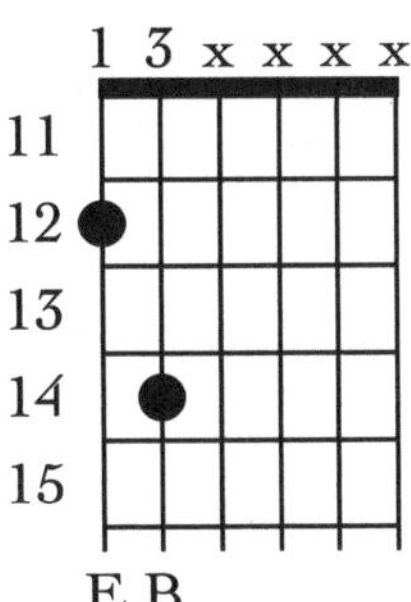
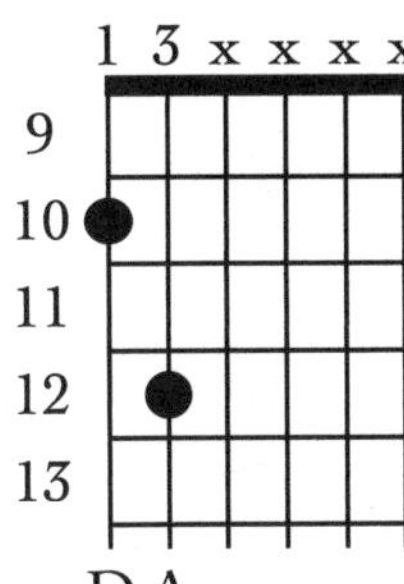

This exercise shows how to harmonize an A Minor Pentatonic scale in parallel 5ths. The tablature shows the low part only. To finger the high part, just play the E Minor Pentatonic scale starting on the 12th-fret E note.

Exercise 62

This example shows how to harmonize a rockin' A blues riff in parallel 5ths. The tablature shows only the low part. To finger the high part, just play the same riff from the E Blues scale at the 12th fret.

Exercise 63

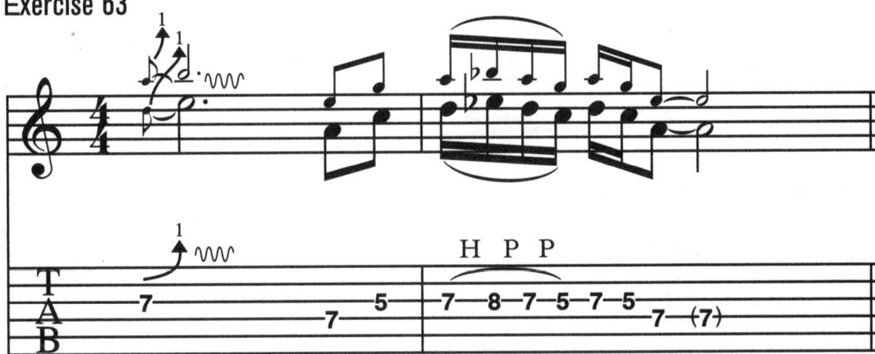

Notes: When a perfect 5th is transposed down one octave it becomes a perfect 4th below the original root note. Of course, the notes in the harmony part are exactly the same. They are just lower than the root, instead of higher. This is a cool sound. You should try it as well.

When using a less expensive harmonizer that does not have the "smart" function, you may wish to set it to harmonize a 5th above, or a 4th below, so that you can play anything from the pentatonic or blues scales in harmony.

CHAPTER 13: FINGER TAPPING

Finger tapping was popularized by Eddie Van Halen in the early 1980s. Van Halen's "Eruption" showcases the technique brilliantly, as does Randy Rhoads's unaccompanied solo in Ozzy Osbourne's live recording of "Suicide Solution." Jennifer Batten recorded "The Flight of the Bumblebee" entirely with tapping. Finger tapping is a comparatively easy way to play rapid-fire legato passages. We hammer on to notes on the neck with right-hand fingers and then pull off to lower notes that are fingered by the left hand. With both hands on the neck, wide interval leaps and amazing speed are made easy. It starts to become much more difficult when more than one right-hand finger taps onto the neck. The following examples start very easy and get harder as they go.

This exercise is in the style of Van Halen's "Eruption." Try it over an A Minor chord.

Exercise 64

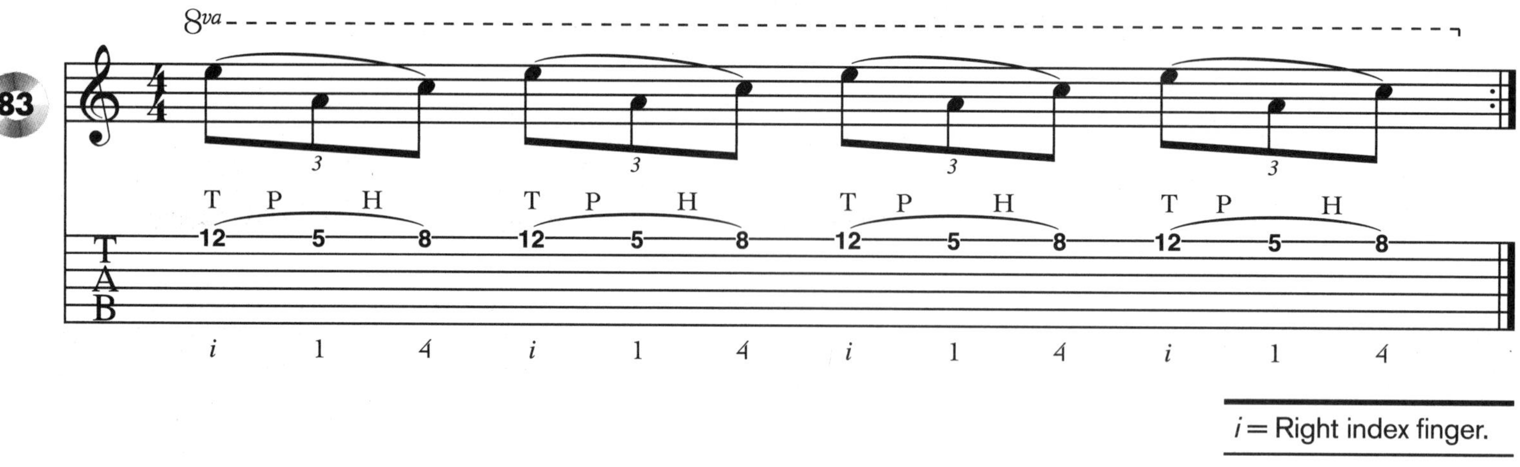

Exercise 65 is in the style of Randy Rhoads's "Crazy Train." This works over an A Minor chord as well.

Exercise 65

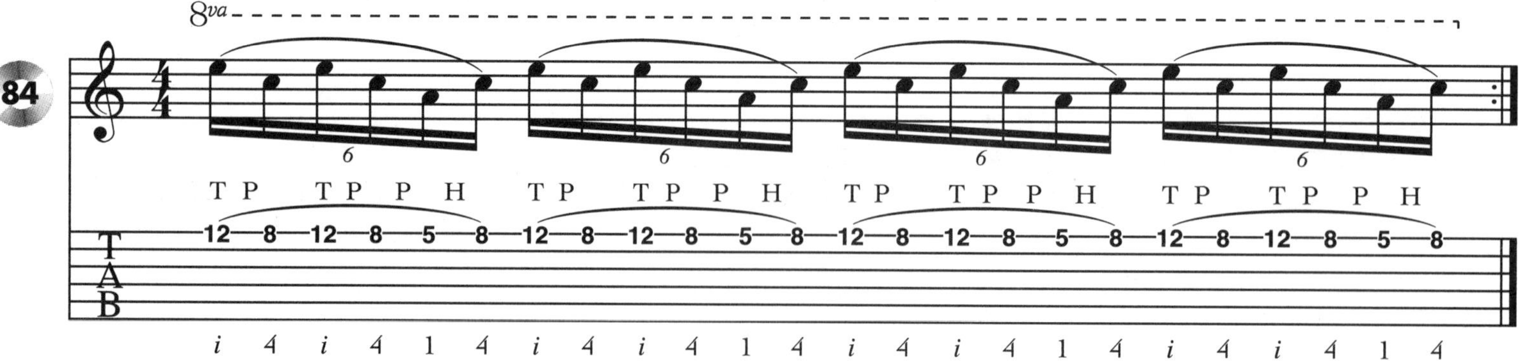

Notice how Examples 64 and 65 "spell out" the notes in the A Minor triad (A–C–E). The notes in any chord can be easily finger tapped. The technique is an excellent vehicle for covering chord changes.

This exercise features quintuplets and is in the style of Eddie Van Halen's solo on Michael Jackson's hit "Beat It." Try it over an F# Minor chord.

Exercise 66

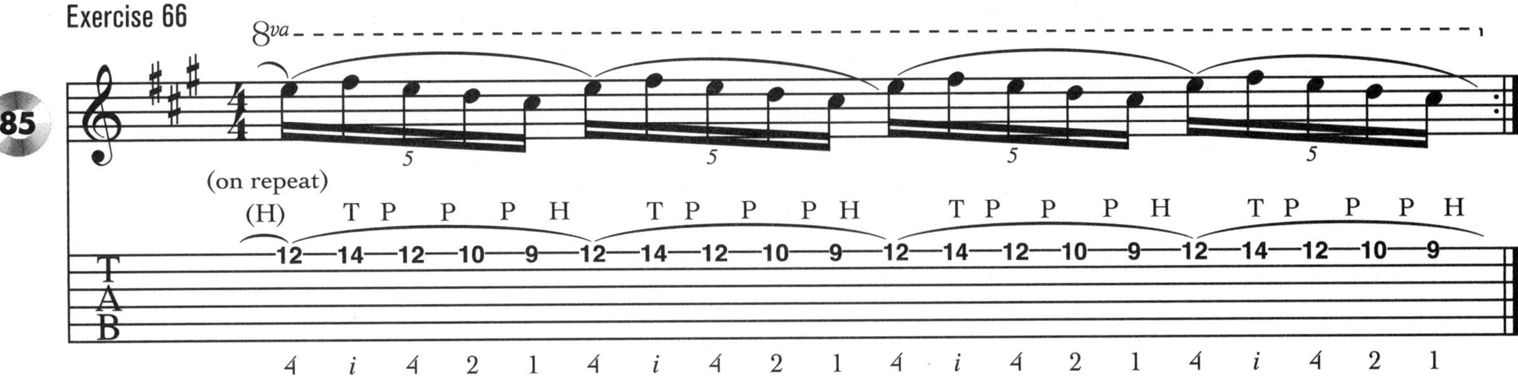

Exercise 67 uses the same concept as above but adds a tapped slide. Tap the 14th fret of the 1st string and then slide the tapping finger along the string to its destination (the 16th fret).

Exercise 67

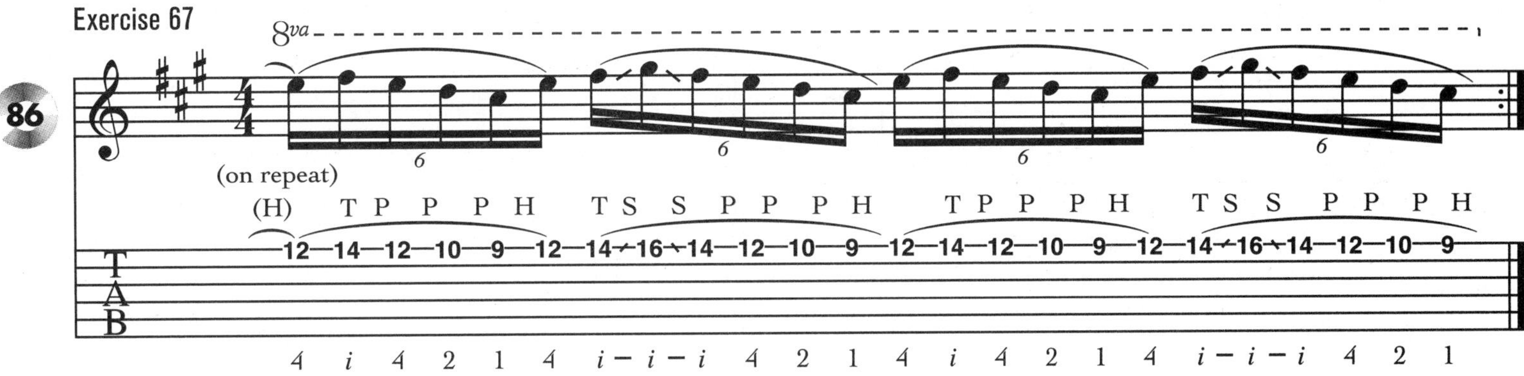

This cool quintuplet riff is in the syle of Van Halen's "Spanish Fly."

Exercise 68

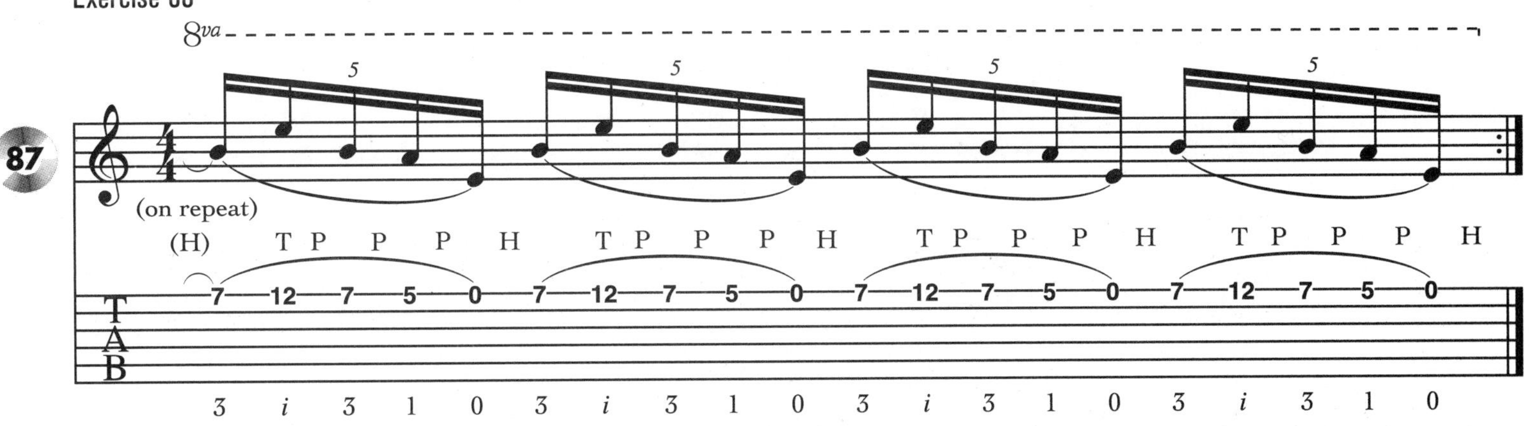

This example sequences the previous concept on two adjacent strings.

Exercise 69

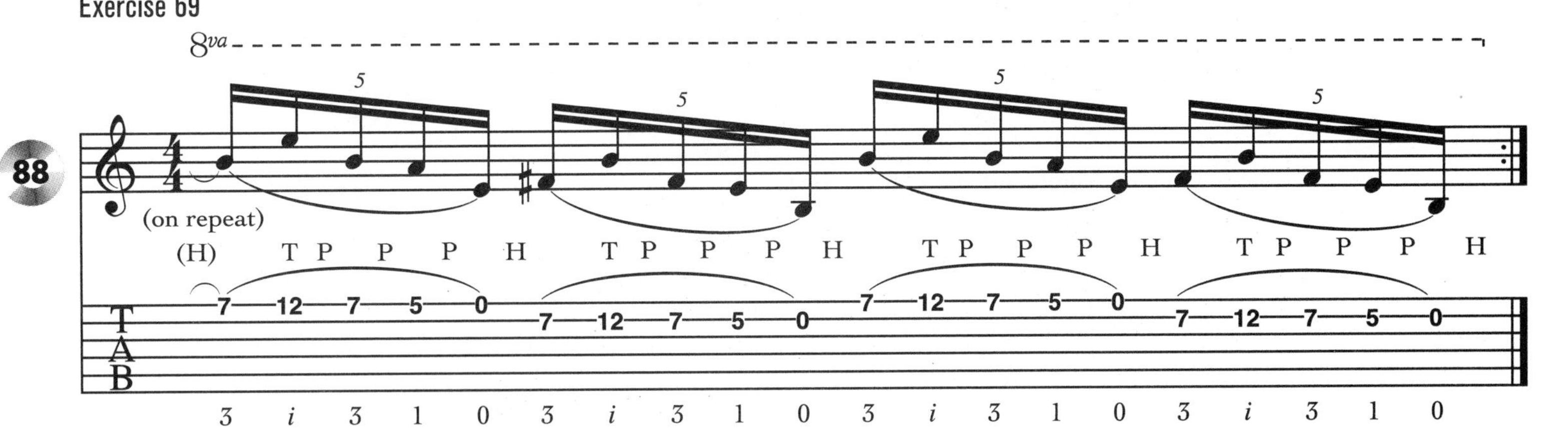

This example uses two right-hand fingers on the neck to arpeggiate a G Minor 7 chord.

Exercise 70

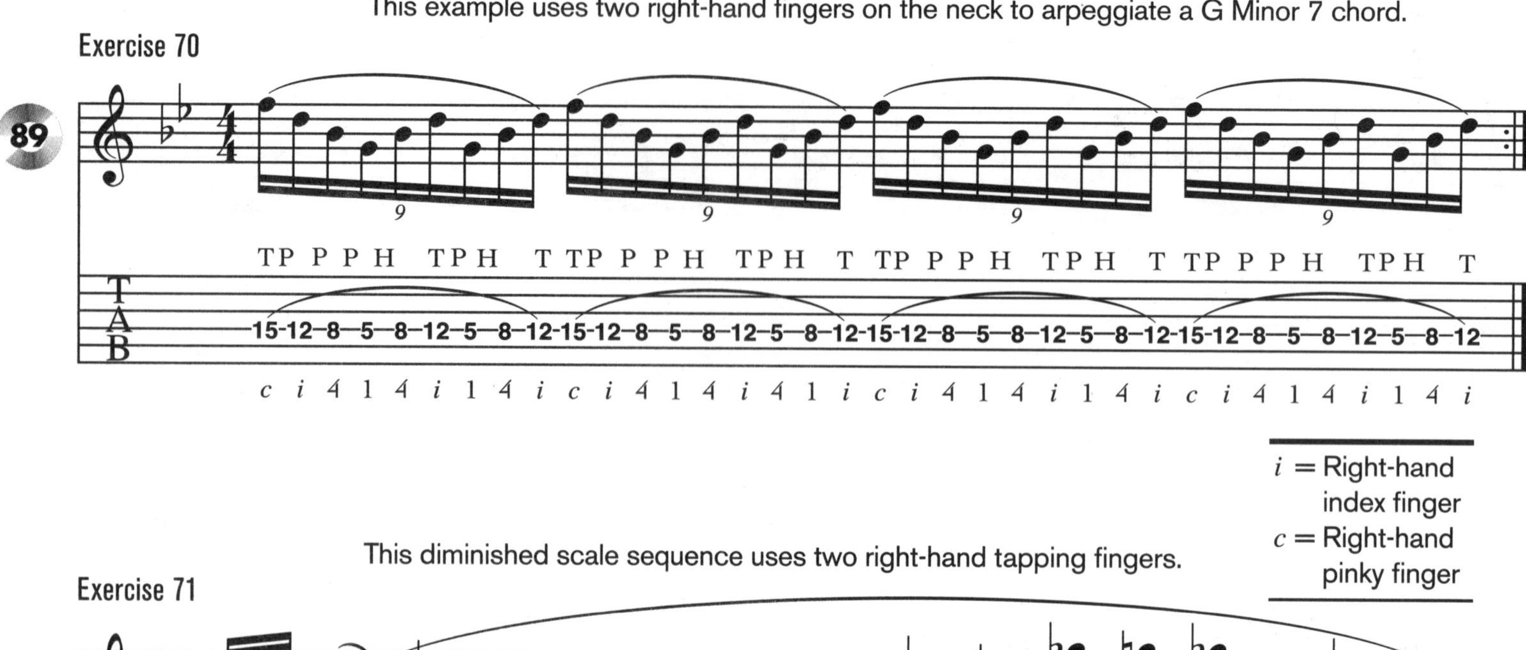

This diminished scale sequence uses two right-hand tapping fingers.

Exercise 71

i = Right-hand index finger
c = Right-hand pinky finger

This example shows a common trick, which is to change a note or two in the riff as it is repeated, which creates an exciting effect. In this case, we change the chord type from minor 7 to major 7.

Exercise 72

Example 73 on page 45 shows how a four-bar "neoclassical" chord progression can be covered with awesome arpeggio and *pedal-tone* riffs (a melodic phrase that alternates between changing notes with static pitches). The tones in each chord and scale are rapidly "spelled out" with tapped notes. This is a useful technique and a simple one to apply to any chord progression. You should try it on your own original tunes or any cover tunes you may be working with. It's a great way to apply your tapping skills!

A Note on Mastering Finger Tapping

Tapping is only one of the many methods used to sound notes on the guitar. Don't let this, or any other technique "run away with you." It's important to try to deliver clear musical ideas with whatever technique you may be using at any given time. You don't want your music to sound like the random by-product of a technique. With that said, there's nothing like the feeling of freely and easily tapping all over the neck using your knowledge of theory, phrasing, and technique. Go for it!

Exercise 73

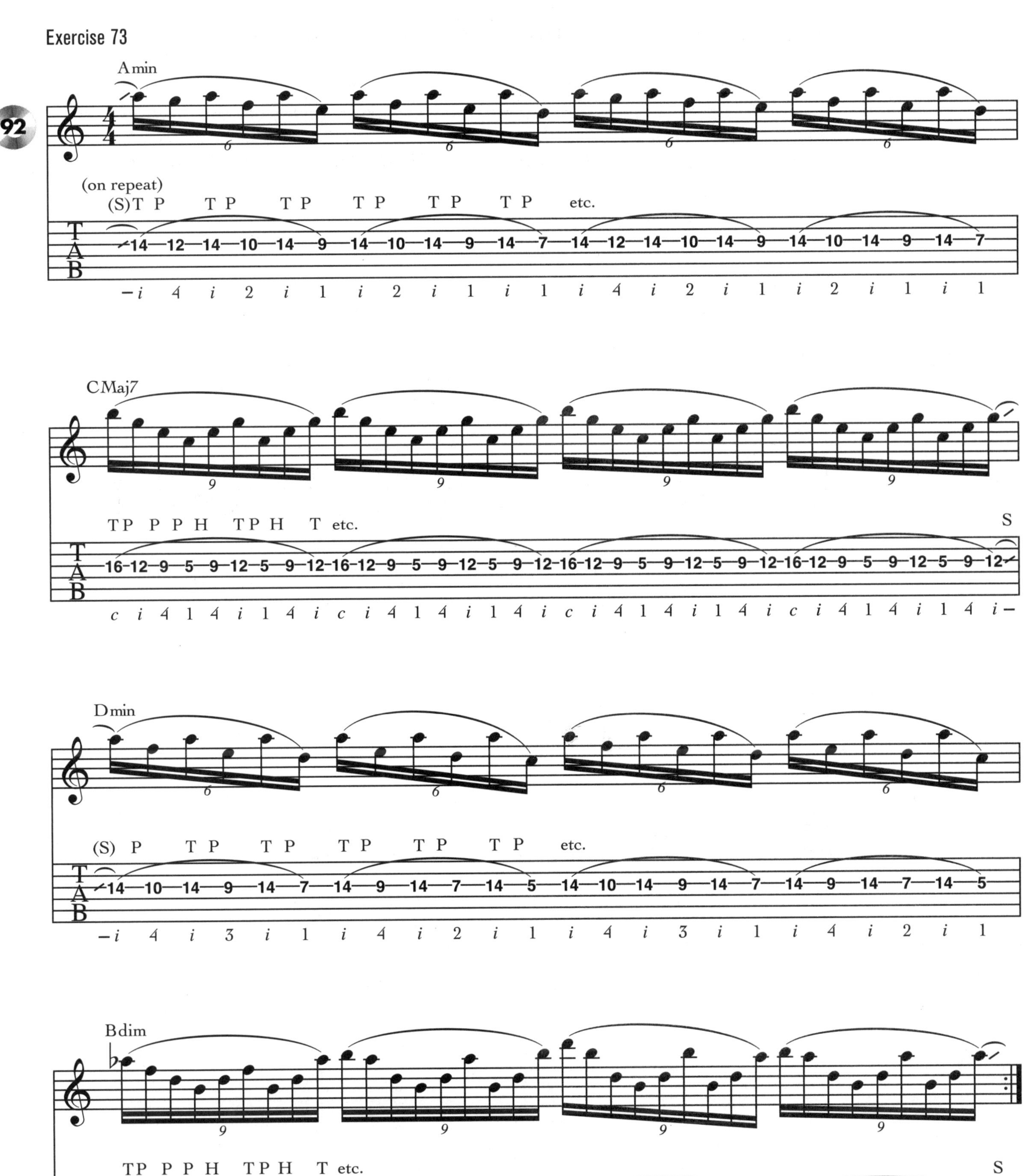

CHAPTER 14: WHAMMY-BAR TECHNIQUES

Does your whammy bar dangle uselessly from your guitar or worse yet, stay out of sight, permanently entombed in your guitar case? Why not use it to play endless creative riffs in the styles of Jimi Hendrix, Steve Vai, Joe Satriani, and others? Many types of vibrato, dive bombs, sirens, grace notes, and other effects can be achieved with a few flicks of the bar. So don't be afraid to "dive" in. The examples here will get you off to a great start.

The "dive bomb" is the most basic and common whammy technique. Just hit a note and depress the bar until the strings are slack. Bombs away!

Exercise 74

= Dive bomb.

This dive bomb resolves to a natural harmonic that is sustained with wide vibrato. Depress the whammy bar enough to lower the pitch an octave and then release it back to the original pitch. You should try this very cool trick over an E Minor chord.

Exercise 75

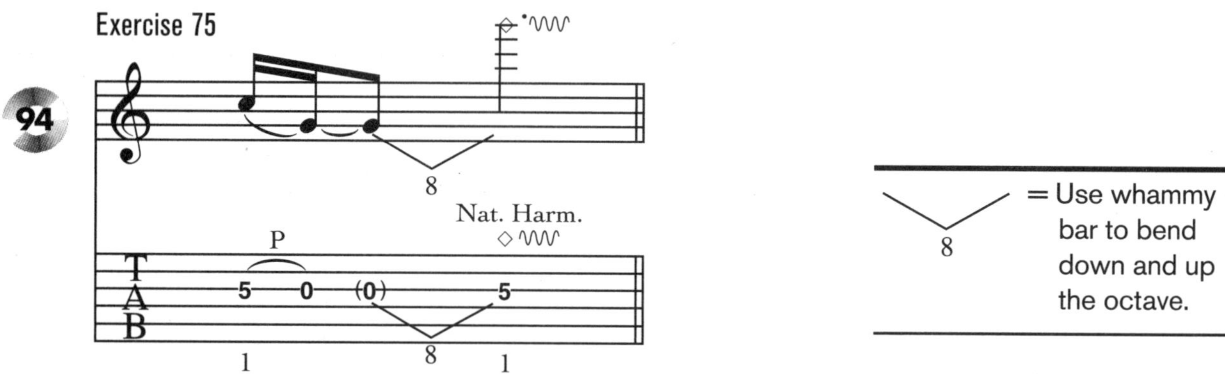

= Use whammy bar to bend down and up the octave.

Exercise 76 is an example of using the whammy bar to manipulate the feedback of a sustained chord. This has been done by Tom Scholz of Boston, Jimi Hendrix, Joe Satriani, and many others.

Exercise 76

With distortion and feedback

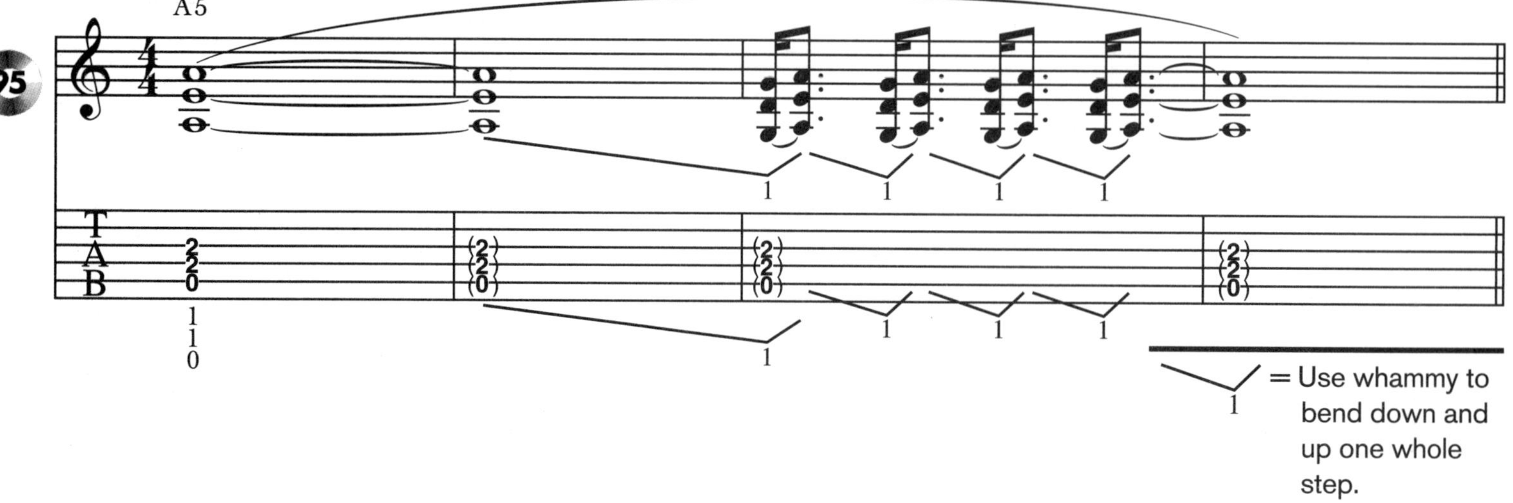

= Use whammy to bend down and up one whole step.

Exercise 77

96

There is no written music for this exercise. It is in the style of Jimi Hendrix and it sounds just like the *Doppler effect* (a change of pitch caused by the source being in motion) of a British police siren. Follow these simple steps to get the sound:

1. Hammer on and pull off rapidly and continuously from E to G, on the 12th and 15th frets of the 1st string.

2. Slowly and steadily depress the bar and then let it return to its normal position while maintaining the trill.

Exercise 78 explores a technique championed by Steve Vai that is often called "chirping the bar." The bar is adjusted so that it stays in one place instead of dangling loosely. Then, the bar is slapped toward the body of the guitar and allowed to snap back to its normal position during a riff. This causes a "poinging" vibrato on the note or notes that are chirped. Vai does this a lot in the song For the Love of God" from his ground-breaking instrumental rock release, *Passion and Warfare*. It sounds awesome, but it only works on guitars with floating tremolo systems.

Exercise 78

97

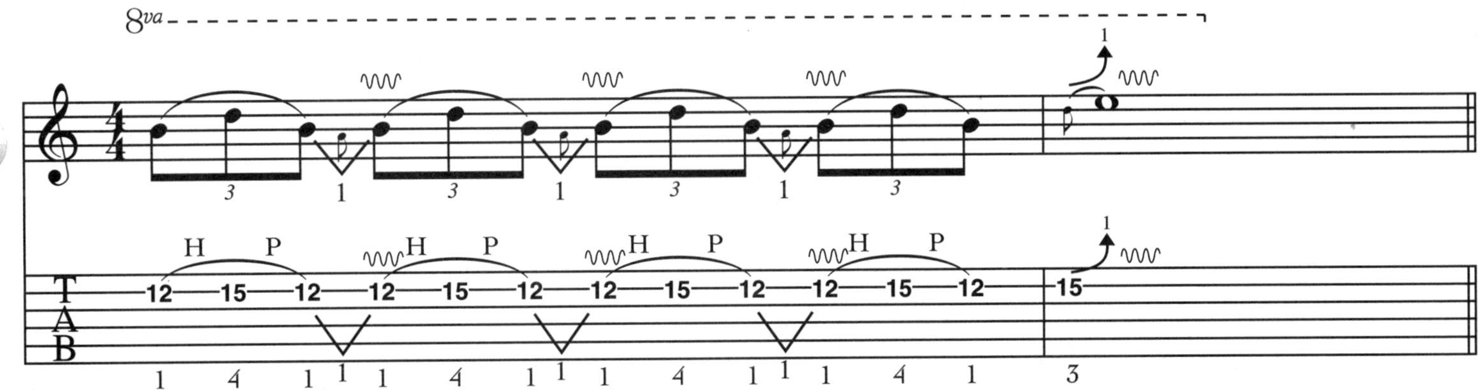

This is another essential shred/metal riff. Here, the bar is used to fuel an ascending passage in A Minor. Instead of picking, hold the bar and dip it right before each hammer-on/pull-off combination. You'll find that the momentum gained by the bar eliminates the need to pick.

Exercise 79

98

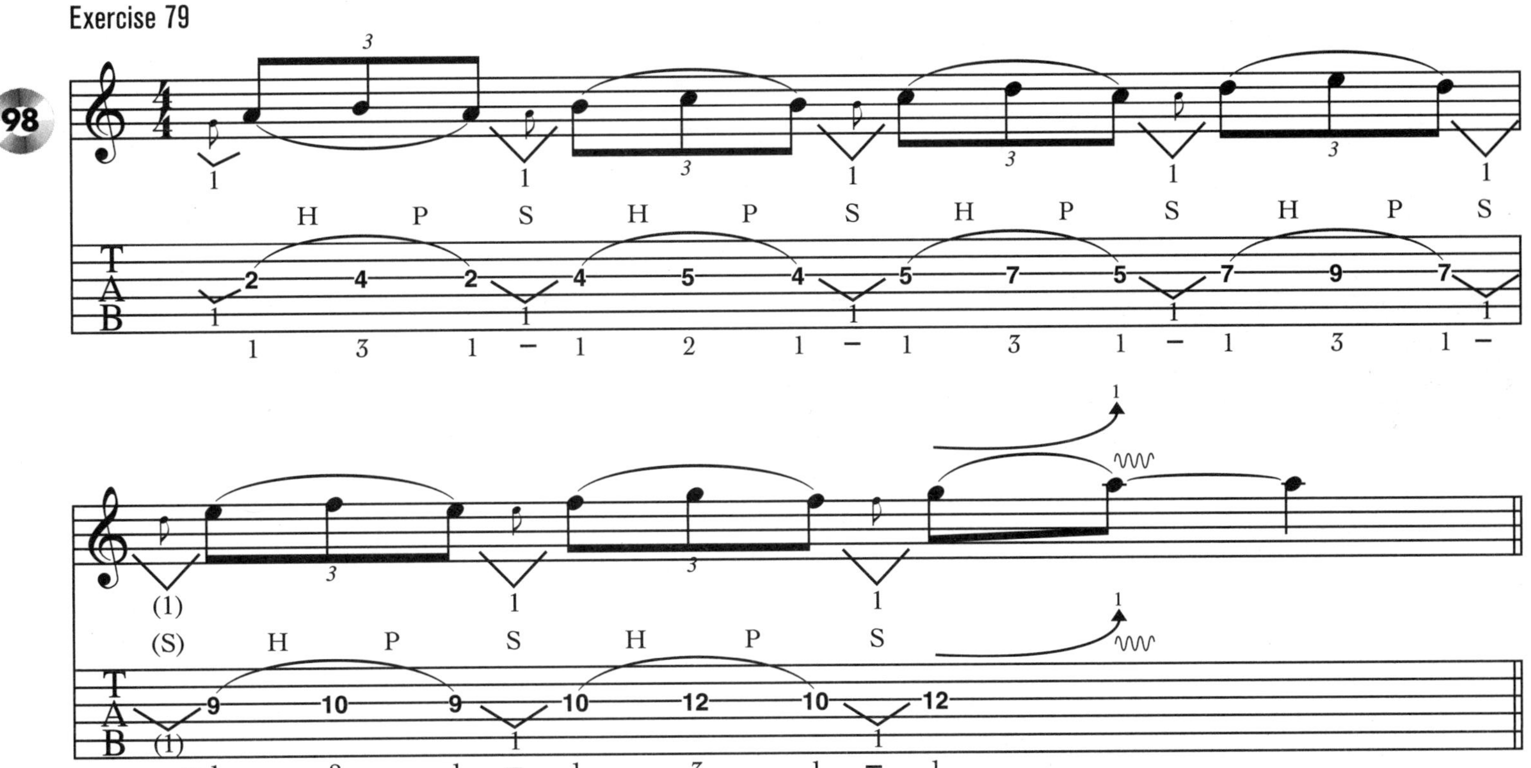

CHAPTER 15: LEGATO

The word *legato* means smooth and connected. Hammer-ons, pull-offs, slides, bends, and finger taps are all techniques that are commonly used to create fluid legato passages. Eddie Van Halen's intro to "Hot for Teacher" and Joe Satriani's improvisations on "Flying in a Blue Dream" are both marvelous examples of legato shredding. The first step toward a great legato technique is mastering hammer-ons and pull-offs, so that's where we'll begin.

This example introduces a *trill* on the 1st string. A trill is a rapid and continuous series of hammer-ons and pull-offs. You should master the basic trill before attempting the rest of the examples in this section.

Exercise 80

Written:

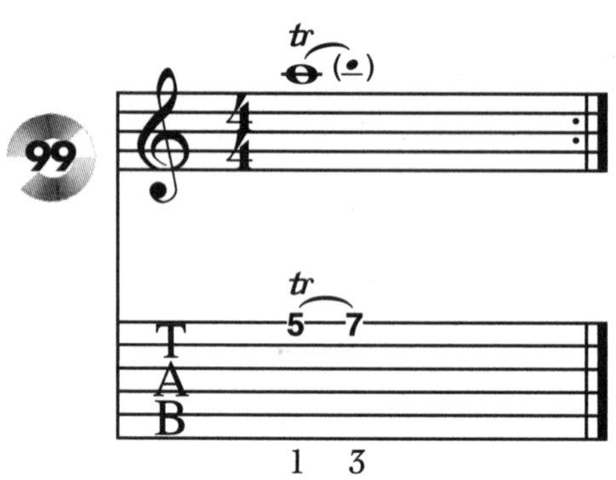

Played:

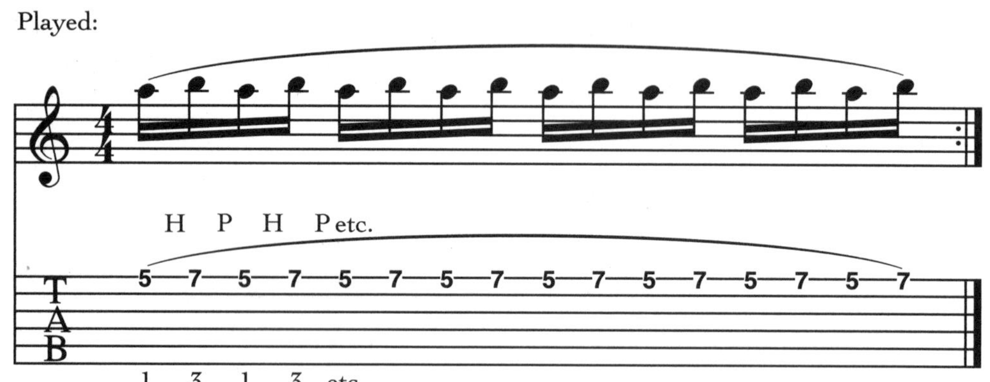

Check out how the legato trill can be moved around on one string, Steve Vai-style, creating an exciting crescendo. Try this riff over a C Minor chord.

Exercise 81

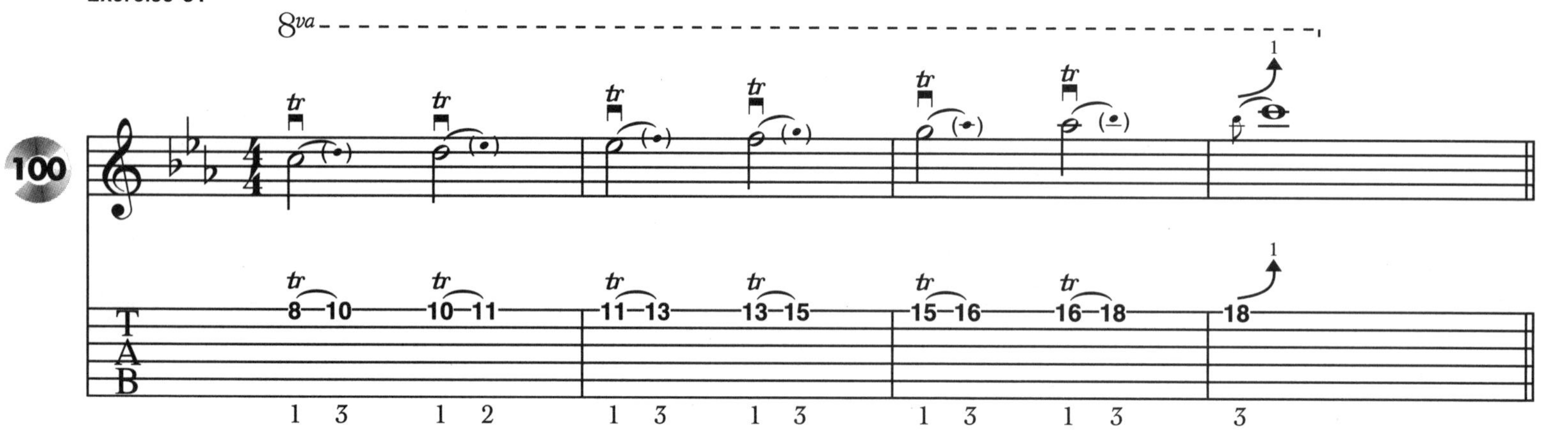

This one is in the style of Randy Rhoads and is an excellent chops-building drill. Try it over a D Major chord.

Exercise 82

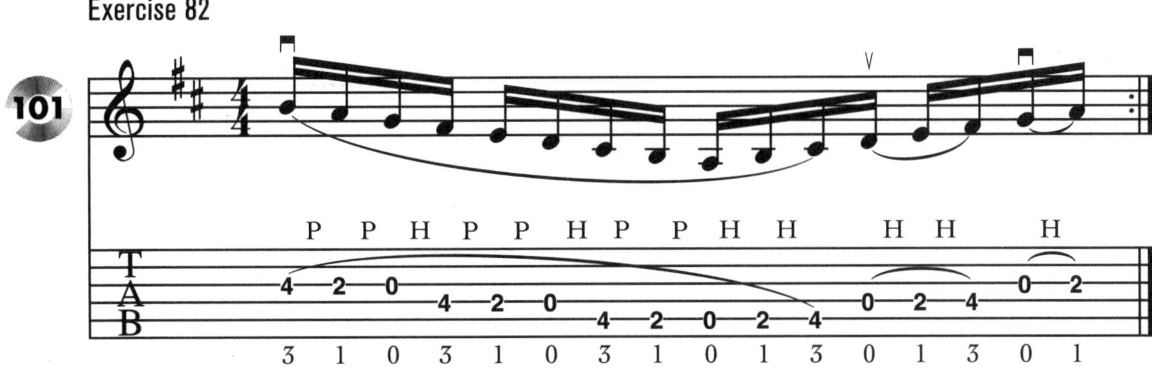

This example shows how a similar idea can be moved up the 3rd string in the key of A Minor.

Exercise 83

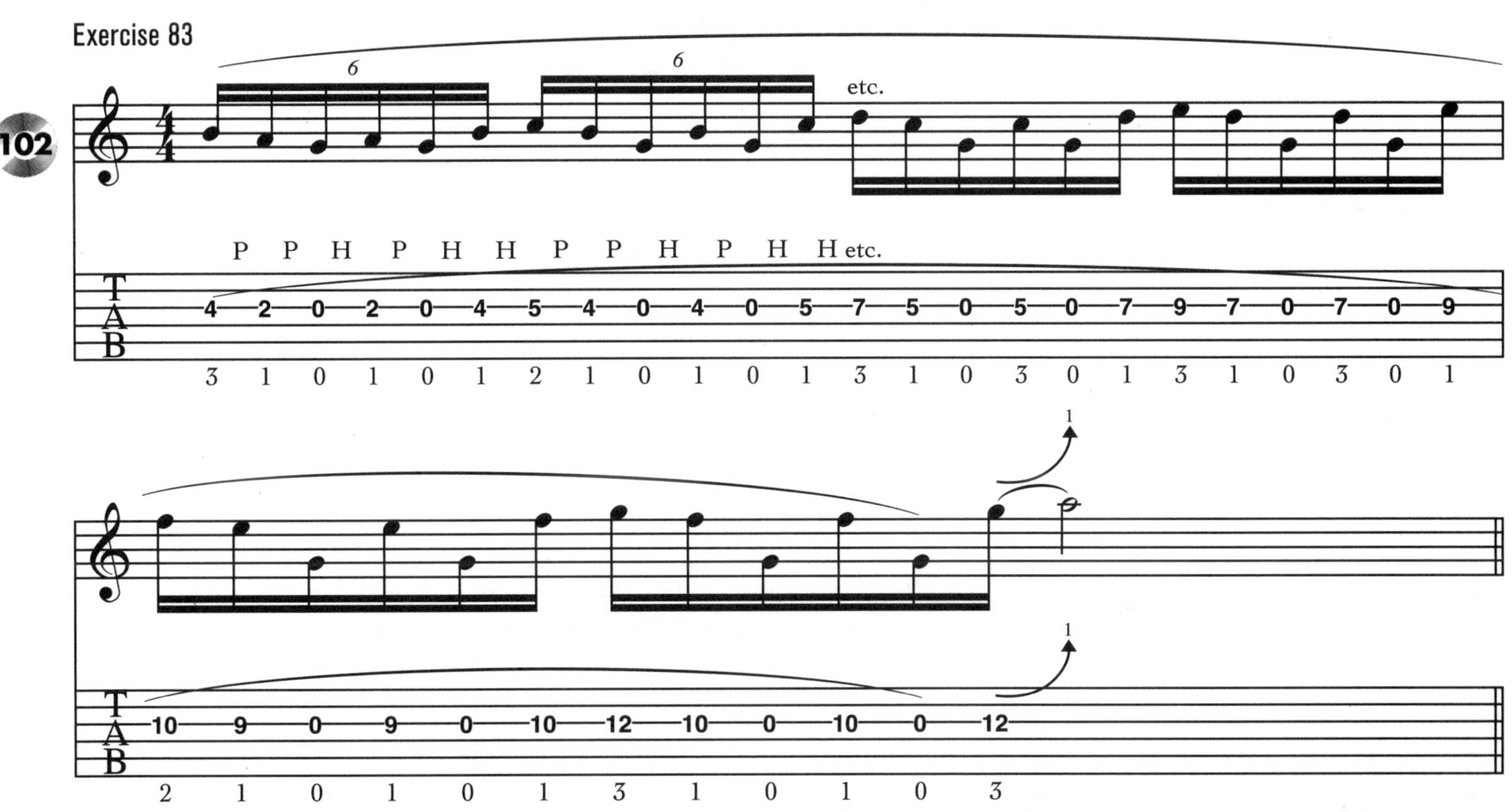

I call this technique "the punk pull-off." Almost every modern punk guitar solo contains this cool legato technique. Check it out!

Exercise 84

This is a very cool legato sequencing technique in the style of Joe Satriani. Try it in the key of E Minor.

Exercise 85

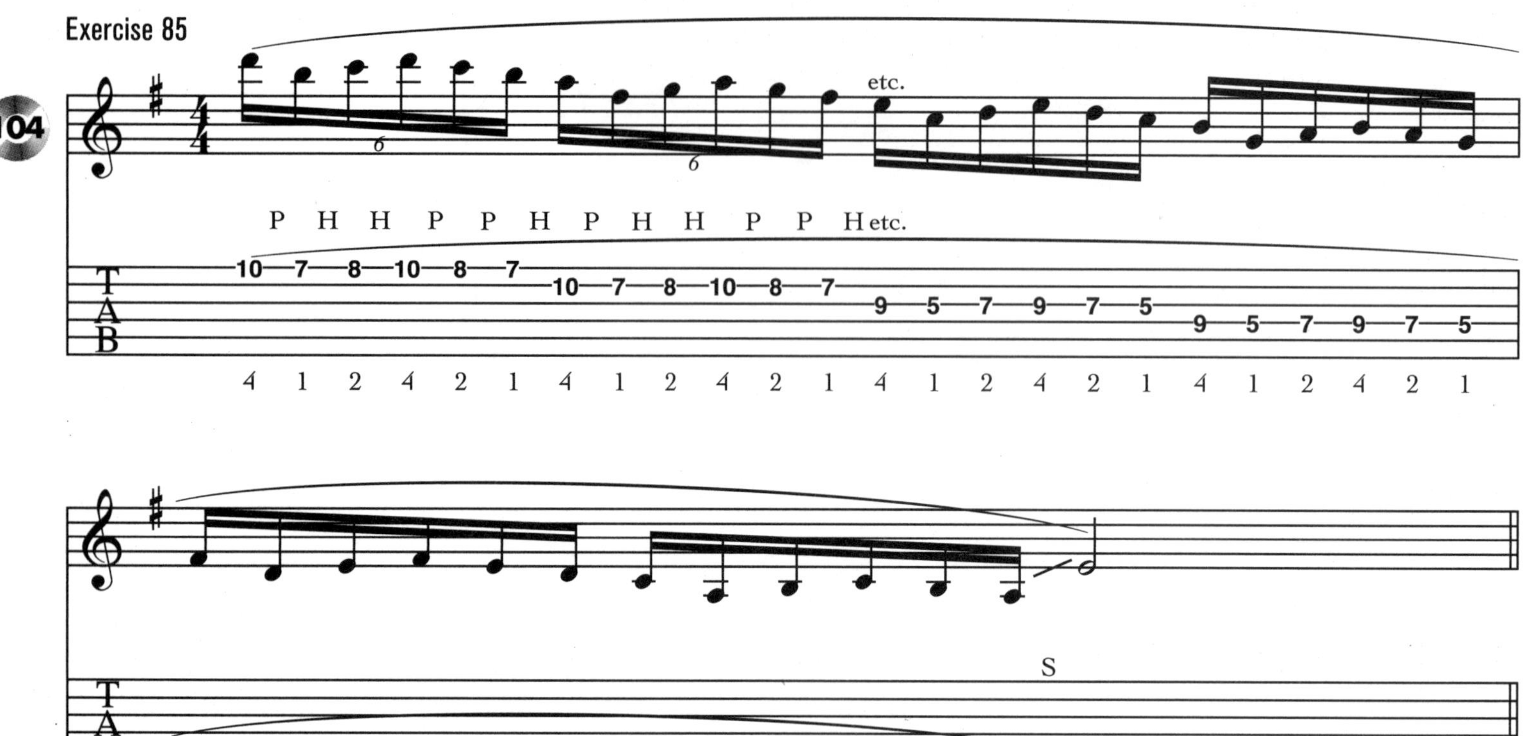

This slippery whole-tone riff can be played unaccompanied or over either an A Augmented chord or A7♯5 chord. For a more advanced version of the same idea, see the Exotic Scales chapter starting on page 55.

Exercise 86

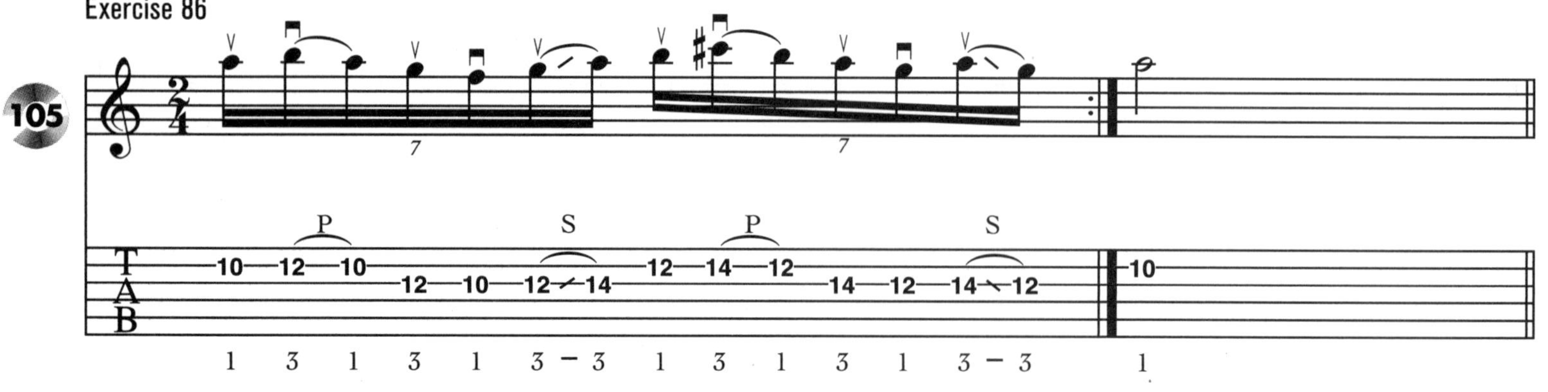

CHAPTER 16: LONG SCALES

Playing scales of three or more octaves is an important chops builder and is an advanced technique. This section will introduce you to several three-octave scale forms, the shifting techniques used to play them, and special techniques used for extending them beyond three octaves.

The Glide Shift

This technique comes from the classical tradition. It is used to smoothly move up or down the neck without sliding. It is essential that the indicated fingerings be used.

Exercise 87

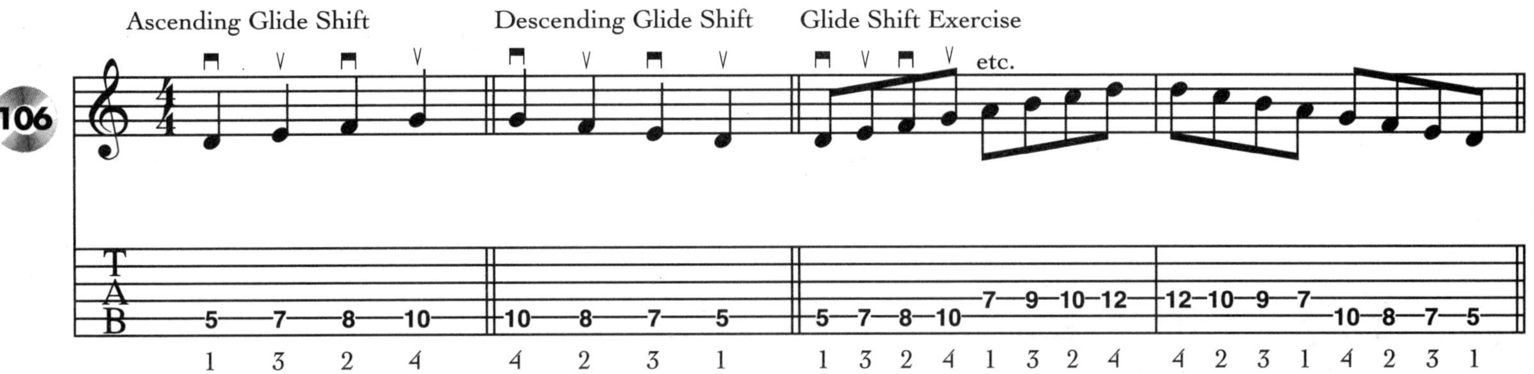

The Leap

This position-shifting technique also comes from the classical tradition. It is used to smoothly navigate the neck without sliding. Follow the fingerings closely.

Exercise 88

The Three-Octave Major Scale Form

Exericse 89 is played in G, although it can be moved to another key simply by starting on another note. Notice the glide shifts and leaps that are used to make the fingerings possible.

Exercise 89

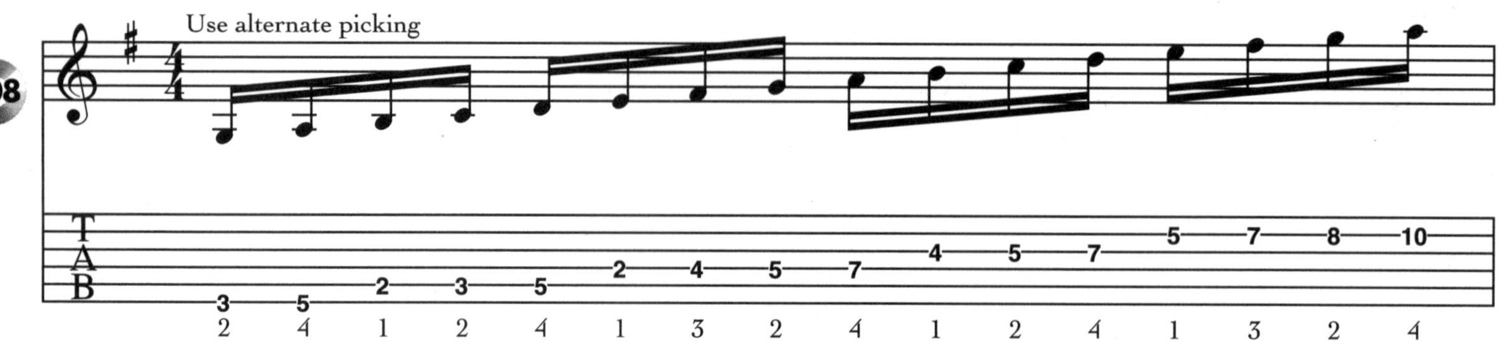

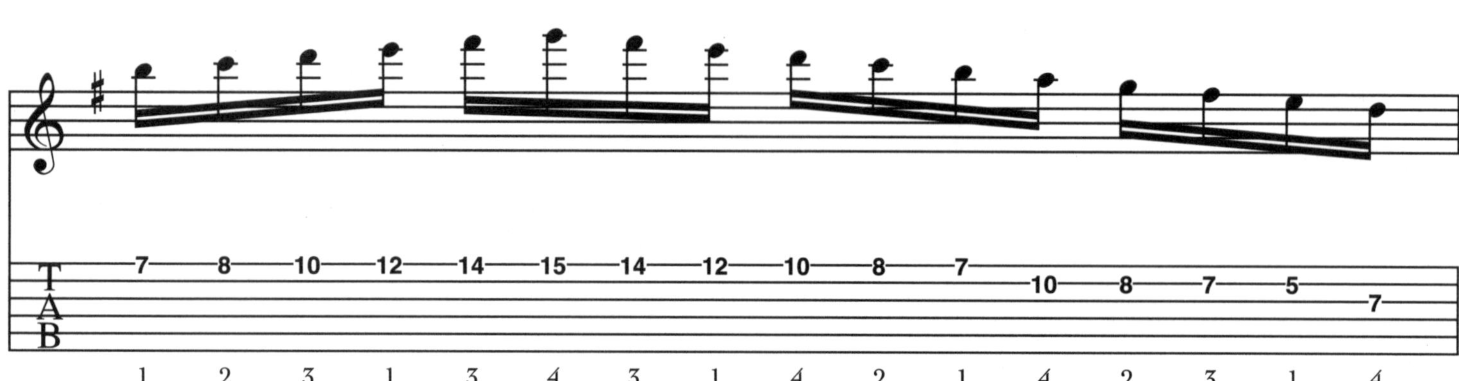

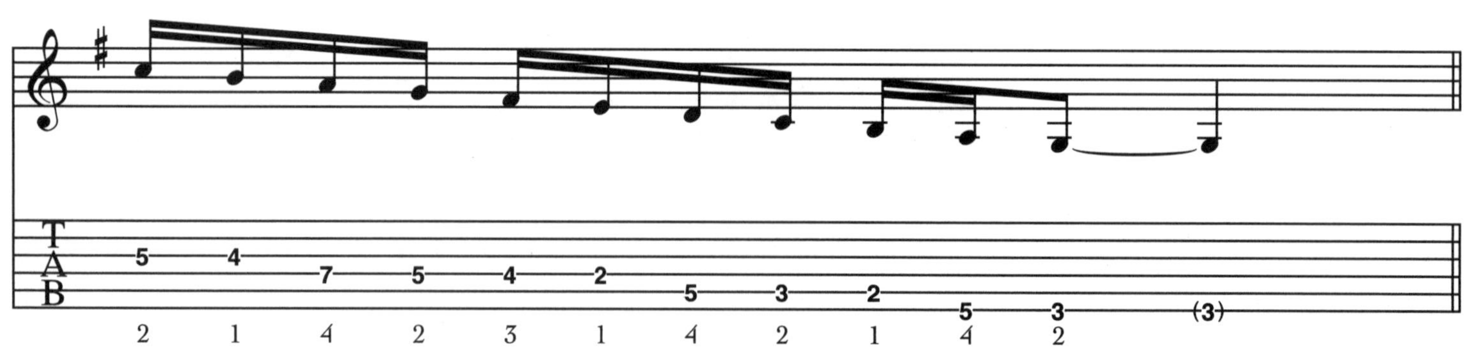

The Three-Octave Minor Scale Form

This exercise is played in A Minor, although it can also be moved to another key simply by starting
on another note. Notice the glide shifts that are used to make the fingerings possible.

Exercise 90

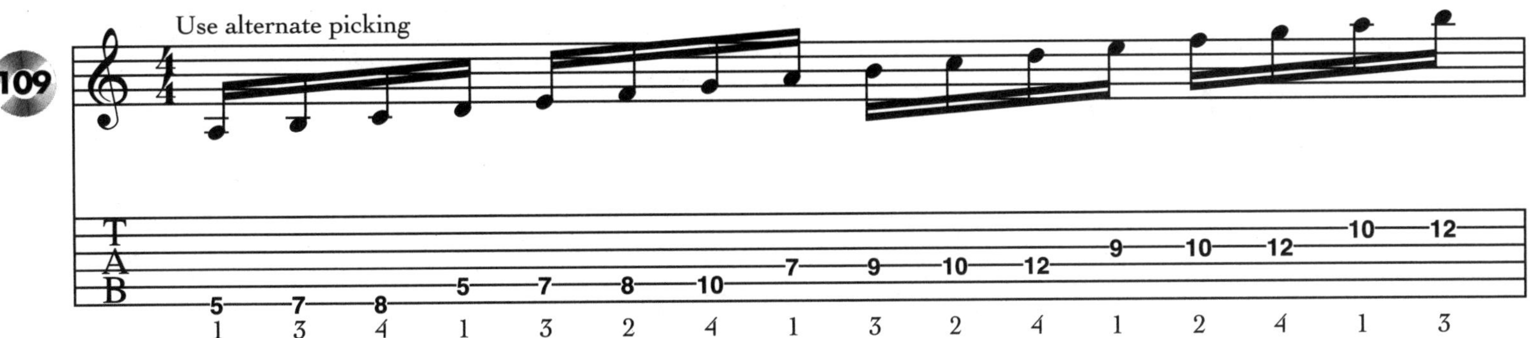

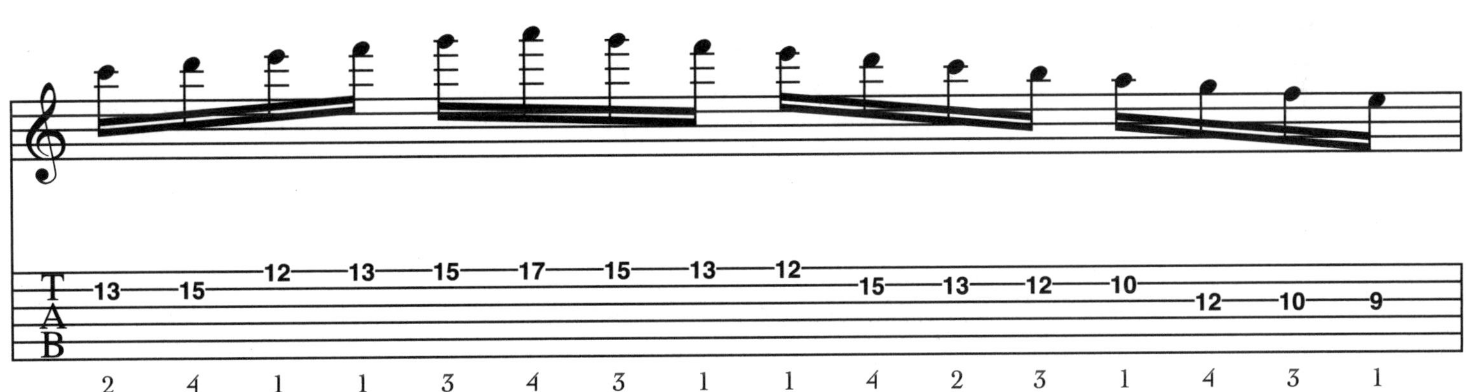

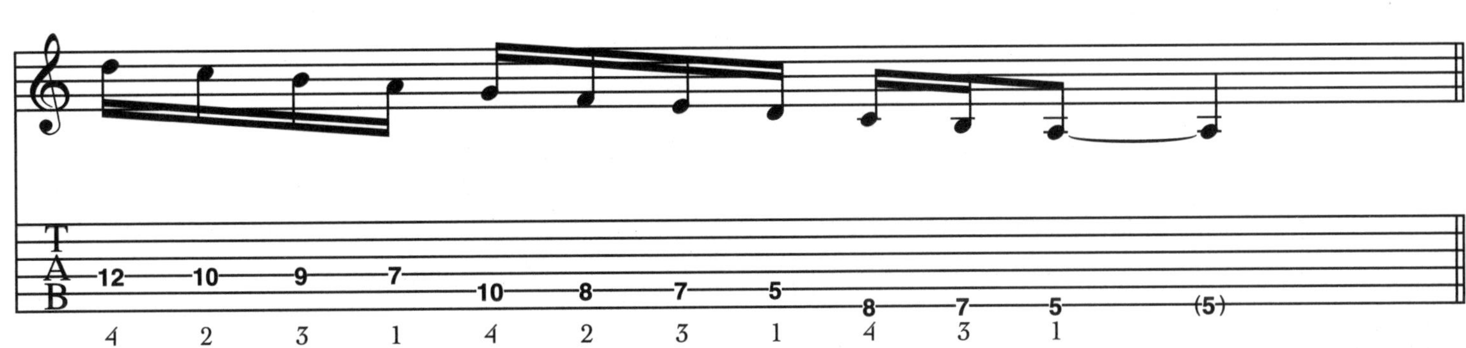

Extensions

Exercise 91 adds the notes E and F♯ to the G Major scale in Exercise 89 on page 52. Play these notes first, then play the G Major scale as written. This extends the scale an extra minor 3rd transforming it into an E Minor scale of slightly more than three octaves.

Exercise 91

This exercise adds the notes E, F, and G to the A Minor scale in Exercise 90 on page 53. Play these notes first, then play the A Minor scale as written. This extends the scale an extra 4th, transforming it into an E Phrygian scale of slightly more than three octaves.

For a smoother position shift, use the open-5th-string A instead of the A on the 6th string, 5th fret.

Exercise 92

Note: To learn another valuable shifting technique, study the last two bars of the Human Sequencer Syndrome arpeggio etude on page 64. This two-bar section features a better than three-octave descending Phrygian natural 3rd scale. This exotic scale is executed with a four-note-per-string fingering in which the 1st finger always shifts to the new, lower position. The four-note-per-string approach allows for smooth, easy alternate picking.

CHAPTER 17: EXOTIC SCALES

Many rock guitarists yearn to break through the boundaries presented by common pentatonic and major scales. This feeling of being trapped within the confines of simple scales is common but the cure is simple: learn to use exotic scales. Ritchie Blackmore, Jimi Hendrix, Yngwie Malmsteen, Keith Richards, George Harrison, Jimmy Page, and even Noodles of The Offspring, have successfully woven exotic scales into rock compositions and improvisations. You can, too. This section contains descriptions of some unusual scales and information about applying many of the exotic scales used in rock. Enjoy!

Minor Scales

The easiest way to escape the major scale rut is to use minor scales. The *natural minor scale* (Scale 1 below, which is also called the Aeolian mode, is not a truly exotic scale. (The formula is 1–2–♭3–4–5–♭6–♭7–1.) It is, however, the most common minor scale in heavy metal music and four of the exotic scales in this section are based on it. Every major scale contains a natural minor scale, which starts on the major scale's 6th degree; This is called its relative minor or Aeolian mode. The major scale and its relative minor always share the same key signature. (See page 77 for more information on modes.) The relative minor of C Major is A Minor. The relative minor of D Major is B Minor, and so on.

There are two other types of minor scales which are considered exotic because they are more than just a recycling of notes in the major key. These scales are called *harmonic minor* and *melodic minor*. The harmonic minor (Scale 2, below) is a natural minor with a natural 7th degree. (The formula is 1–2–♭3–4–5–♭6–♮7–1.) The melodic minor (Scale 3 on page 56) is just like natural minor with natural 6th and 7th degrees. (The formula is 1–2–♭3–4–5–♮6–♮7–1.) This is sometimes called the jazz minor scale because in classical theory, the melodic minor descends differently (as a natural minor scale) than it ascends.

The natural minor scale (Aeolian mode) is very common in rock and uses the same notes that are found in its relative major scale, which in this case is C Major.

Exercise Scale 1—A Natural Minor

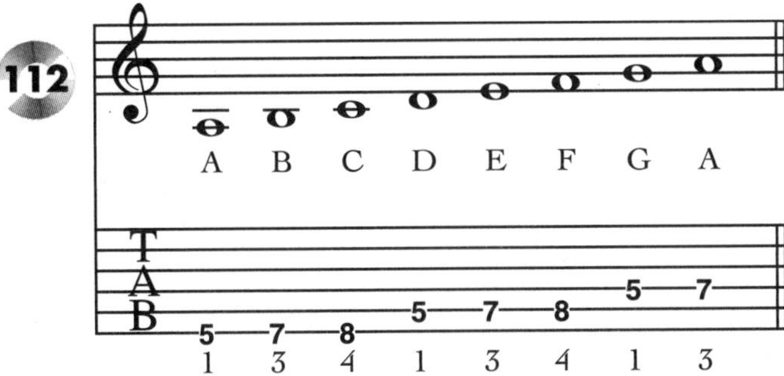

The harmonic minor scale is truly exotic sounding and is used often by neoclassical shredders such as Yngwie Malmsteen. Notice the augmented 2nd interval (one-and-a-half steps) between F and G♯. This is what creates the exotic sound (see page 74 for five harmonic minor scale forms).

Exercise Scale 2—A Harmonic Minor

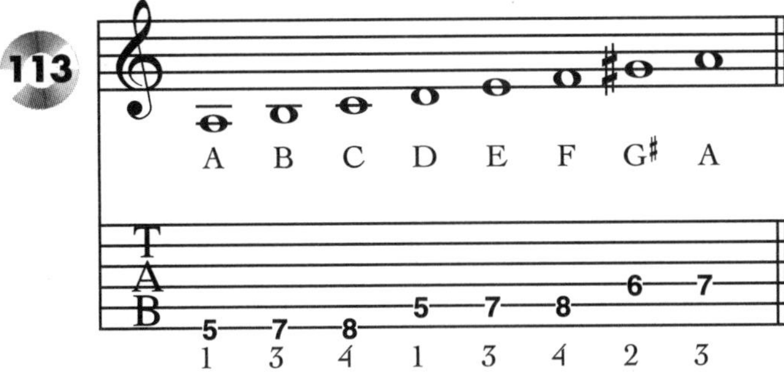

The melodic minor scale, or jazz minor, is exactly like a major scale with a ♭3rd. Several modes of this scale, such as the "Super Locrian" and "Lydian ♭7" are favored by jazz and fusion players.

Scale 3—A Melodic Minor

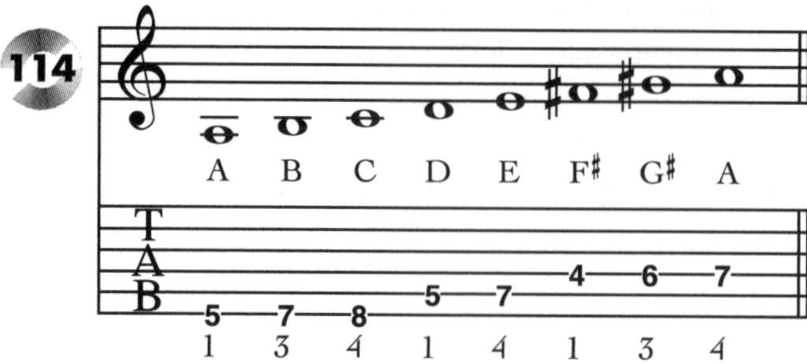

Exotic Modes

The Phrygian ♭3 scale, also called the "Phrygian Dominant," has a very Spanish quality and was used by Jimi Hendrix during his unaccompanied Woodstock solo. This is the 5th mode of the harmonic minor scale. Start the harmonic minor scale on its 5th degree and play to the same note one octave higher. The formula is 1–♭2–3–4–5–♭6–♭7–1.

Scale 4—Phrygian ♭3

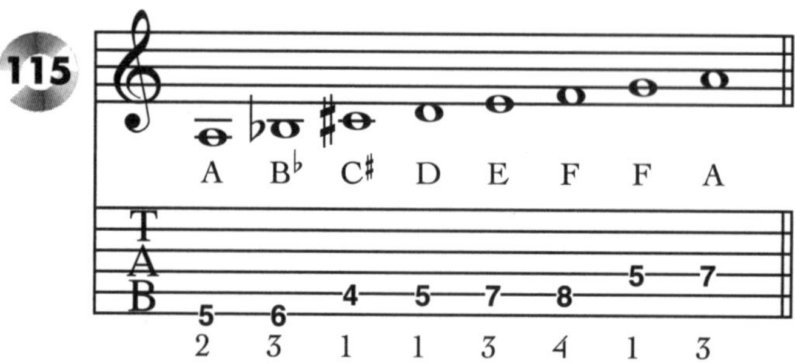

This jazzy scale is the 7th mode of the melodic minor scale. It is commonly used to improvise over *altered dominant chords* (dominant chords with altered extensions, such as E7♯9). Start the melodic minor scale on its 7th degree and play to the same note one octave higher. The formula is 1–♭2–♭3–♭4–♭5–♭6–♭7–1.

Scale 5—Super Locrian

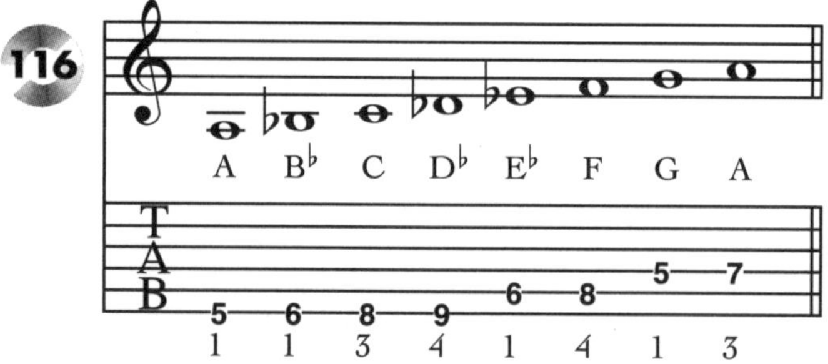

This is the 4th mode of the melodic minor scale. It has a very haunting and exotic sound and can be used to improvise over altered dominants. Start the melodic minor scale on its 4th degree and play to the same note one octave higher. The formula is 1–2–3–♯4–5–6–♭7–1.

Scale 6—Lydian ♭7

Symmetrical Scales

This is a symmetrical scale in which each note is one half step apart with all 12 tones represented. Chromatic tones can be added to any riff or scale for an exotic effect, or the scale can stand alone as a tool for neoclassical or jazz improvisation. "The Flight of the Bumblebee," featured on page 66, is an excellent example of chromatic scales in action. The formula for scale 7 is 1–#1–2–#2–3–4–#4–5–#5–6–#6–7–8.

Scale 7 — Chromatic Scale

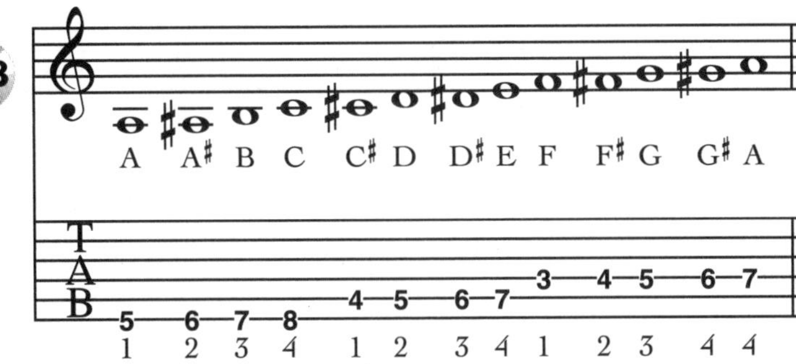

In this six-note scale, all of the notes are one whole step apart. Interestingly, half of the 12 tones are generated, and starting the scale one half step higher will generate the other half. Because of this, when playing a whole tone scale, half of the notes on your fretboard will be in the key and the other half will not. This facilitates some very interesting symmetrical shapes and patterns. Use it over an augmented triad or dominant 7#5 chord. The formula here is 1–2–3–#4–6–♭7–1.

Scale 8—Whole Tone Scale

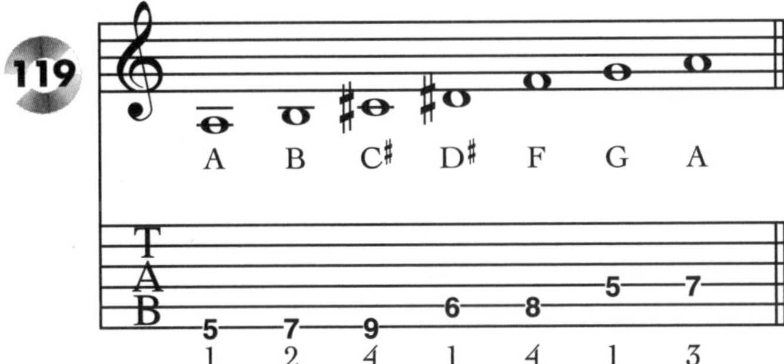

This eight-note scale runs in a symmetrical pattern of whole steps and half steps. There are two diminished scale types which function similarly. One starts on the whole step. The other starts on the half step. These scales can be used over diminished or minor chords. Also, try starting the scale on the 3rd of a dominant 7 chord for a special exotic effect. Interestingly, the A Diminished scale contains the same notes as the C, E♭, and G♭ Diminished scales. The formula is 1–2–♭3–4–♭5–♭6–♭♭7*–♭1–1.

Scale 9 — Diminished Scale

* ♭♭ = *Double flat.* Lower the note one whole step.

Try this A Whole Tone scale study for an interesting taste of an exotic scale in action.

Exercise 93

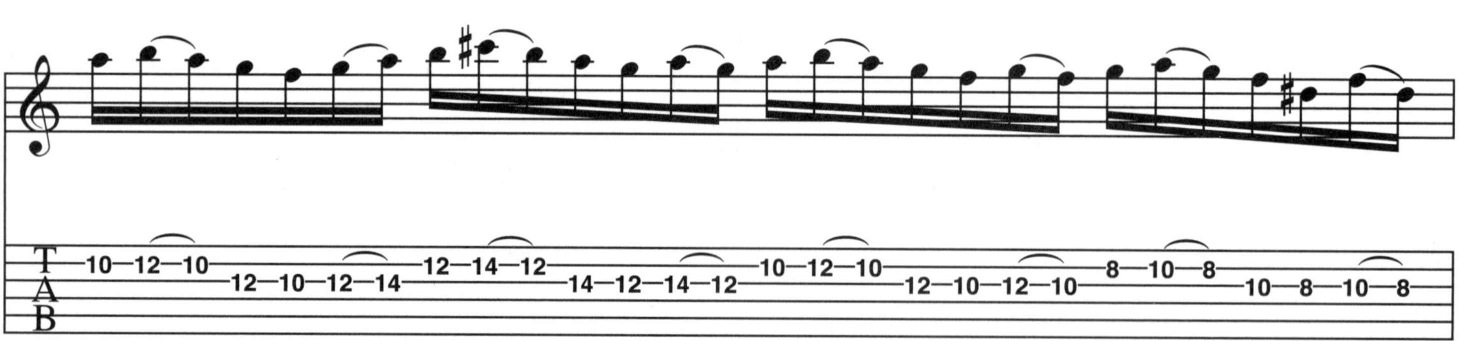

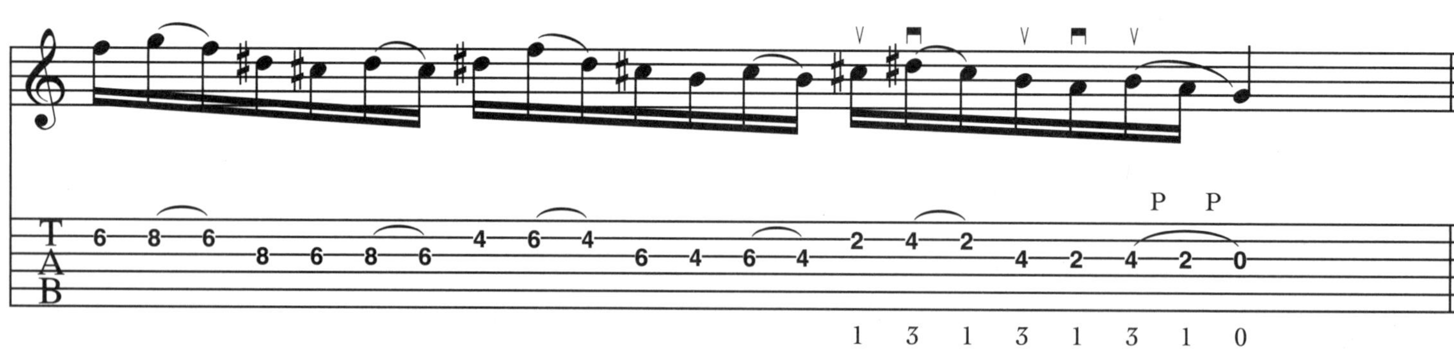

For more exotic scale riffs and studies, see pages 13 (diminished scale study), 19 (diminished arpeggio study), 25 (trem picking Phrygian natural 3rd), 44 (neoclassical finger tapping), 50 (whole tone riff), 61 (diminished arpeggio string skipping), 63 (arpeggio study that includes a greater than three-octave descending harmonic minor scale), 66 ("The Flight of the Bumblebee") featuring lots of chromatic scales), and 74 (five forms of the harmonic minor scale).

CHAPTER 18: HARMONICS

Artificial/Pinch Harmonics

Ever since Billy Gibbons's screeching solo on ZZ Top's "Tush," artificial harmonics (also known as pinch harmonics) have been mainstream rock 'n' roll ear candy. These are different from natural harmonics, which result from manipulating open strings, and can be heard on Yes's "Roundabout" and Metallica's "Nothing Else Matters." An artificial harmonic is one that results from manipulating a string which has a fretted note. You can hear them on just about anything by Steve Vai, Eddie Van Halen, or Zakk Wylde.

Exercise 94

Follow these simple steps to get a pinch harmonic two octaves above the note you are fretting. (See picture.)

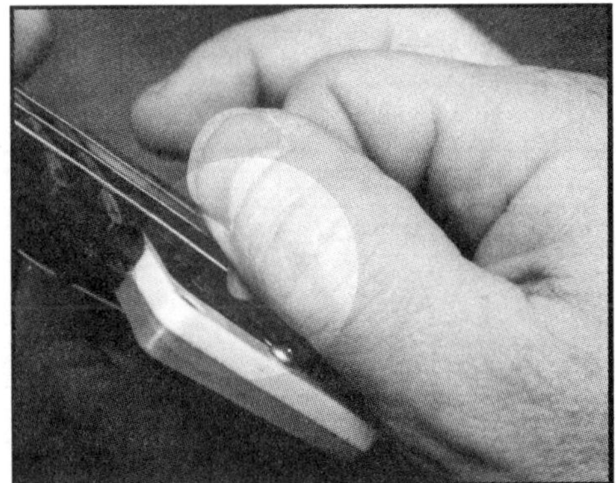

Find the sweet spot, pick there and let the string bounce back into your thumb.

1. Fret any note with your left hand.

2. Locate the spot on the same string that is two octaves (24 frets higher) than the fretted note. This will be beyond the end of your fretboard.

3. Pick that spot with a downstroke and allow the string to snap back and touch your thumb at exactly that spot on the string.

Tips

- *Pinch harmonics work on any guitar, even unplugged, but they work best on electric guitars with humbuckers set to metal distortion.*

- *The "sweet spot" that yields the harmonic may take some trial and error to find. Different sweet spots will produce harmonics that are a 3rd, 5th, b7th or octave away from the original note.*

Try mixing some pinch harmonics into a scale or riff next time you pick up your guitar!

The Natural Harmonic Cascade

Exercise 95

Play a very fast and continuous triplet slur on any string. Use hammer-ons, pull-offs, and three-notes-per-string.

1. Lightly touch the string about two inches from the bridge with your right-hand pinky.

2. While maintaining light pressure with your right hand and continuing to slur, move your pinky toward the body of the guitar.

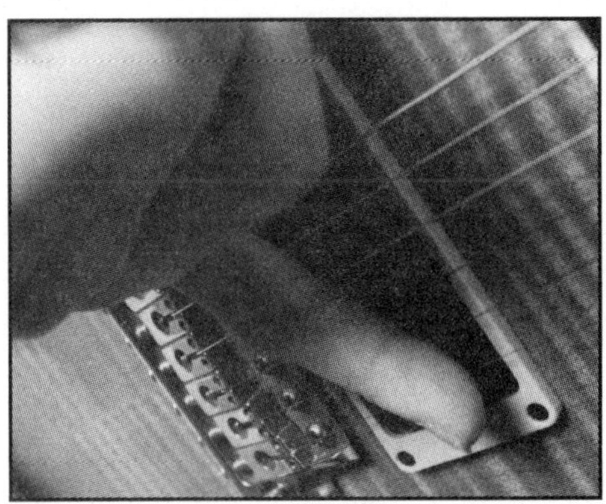

Lightly touch the string about two inches from the bridge with your right- hand pinky.

CHAPTER 19: STRING SKIPPING

String skipping is an advanced picking technique that is frequently used by players like Steve Vai and Eric Johnson. Picking a single string is easy because there is no string shifting involved. Shifting to an adjacent string is simple enough but larger shifts that skip a string or two can be much more difficult. The unusual textures and flamboyant riffs that result from string skipping are well worth the effort it takes to master the technique. The following exercises should get you off to a good start.

Exercise 96 is a good starter exercise for string skipping. The riff will work nicely over C Major or any of its related modes. Start slowly and play accurately.

Exercise 96

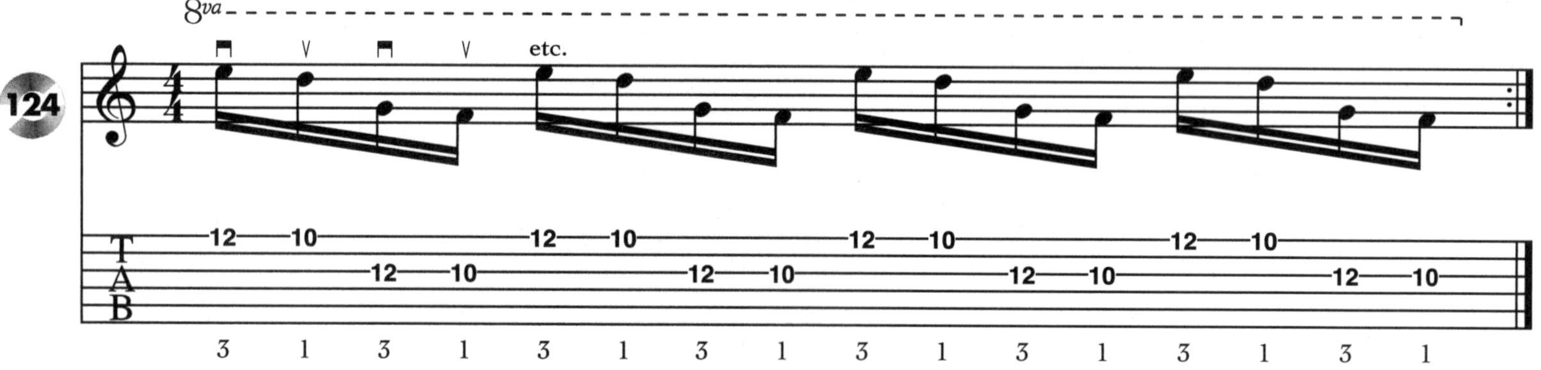

This jazz/rock riff takes the same concept across all of the strings and solidly into the D Dorian mode. Try it over a D Minor chord.

Exercise 97

Here we go with an exciting diminished arpeggio sequence in the style of Yngwie Malmsteen.
Try it over A Minor or A Diminished.

Exercise 98

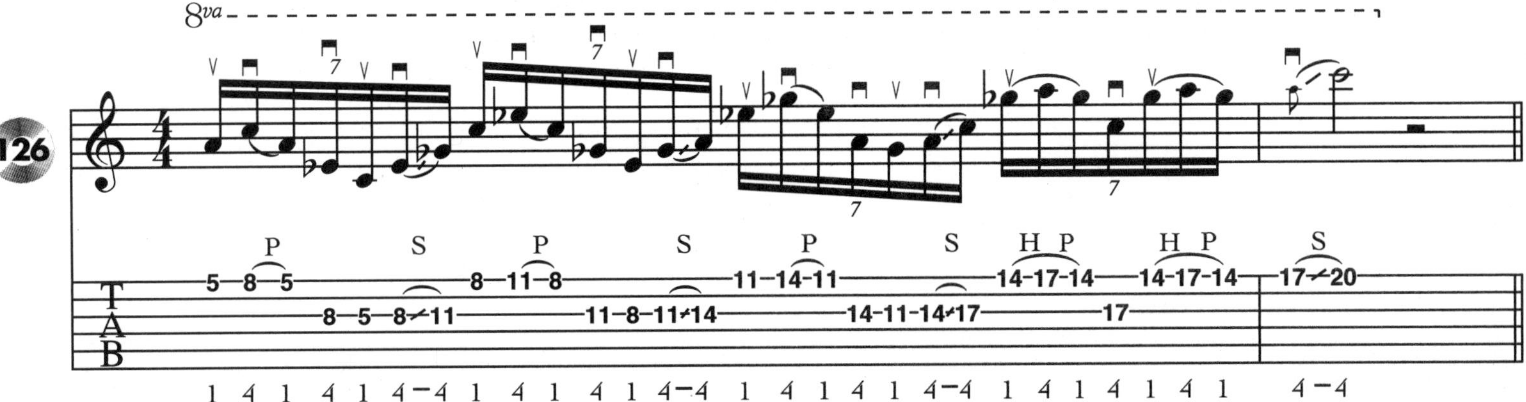

This G Major pedal-tone riff is in the style of Eric Johnson's unaccompanied intro to "Cliffs
of Dover." The lick continuously returns to the G pedal tone as the string skips become wider
and wider.

Exercise 99

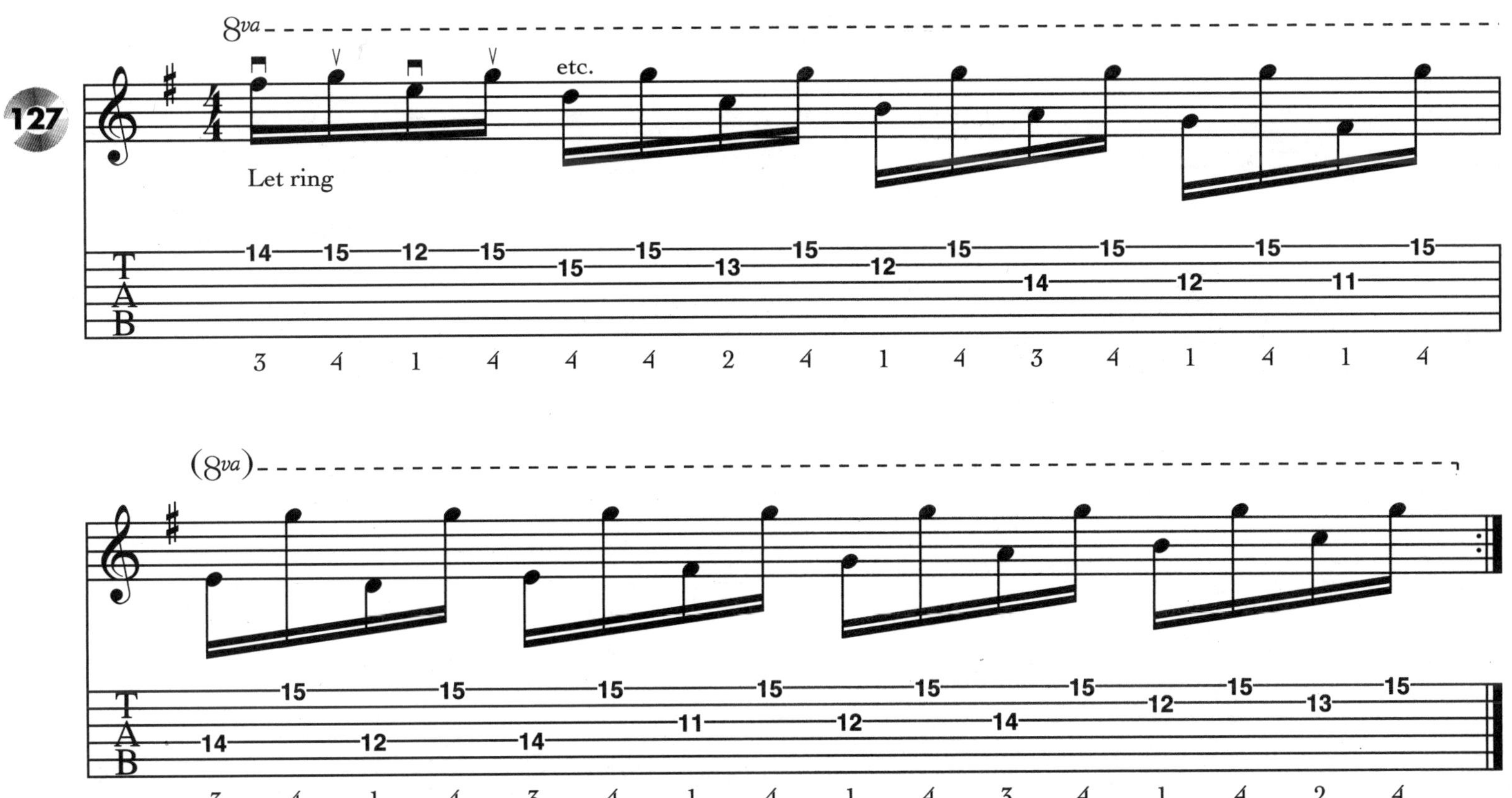

This C Major scale sequence is an excellent string-skipping chops builder. The sequence is commonly referred to as "diatonic 6ths" because it climbs through the scale in 6th intervals.

Exercise 100

128

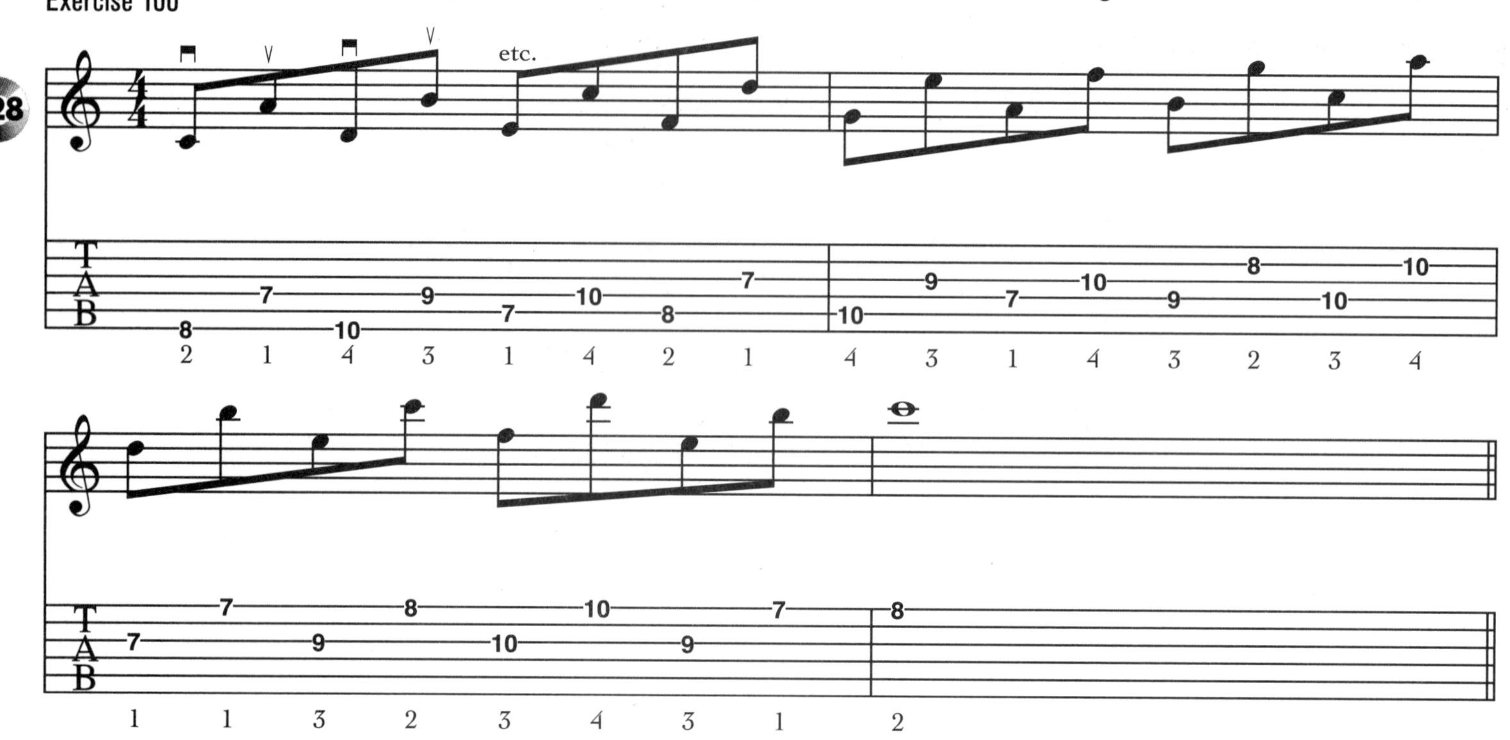

This D Dorian string-skipping workout features the widest possible string leaps, from low E to high E. Go for it!

Exercise 101

129

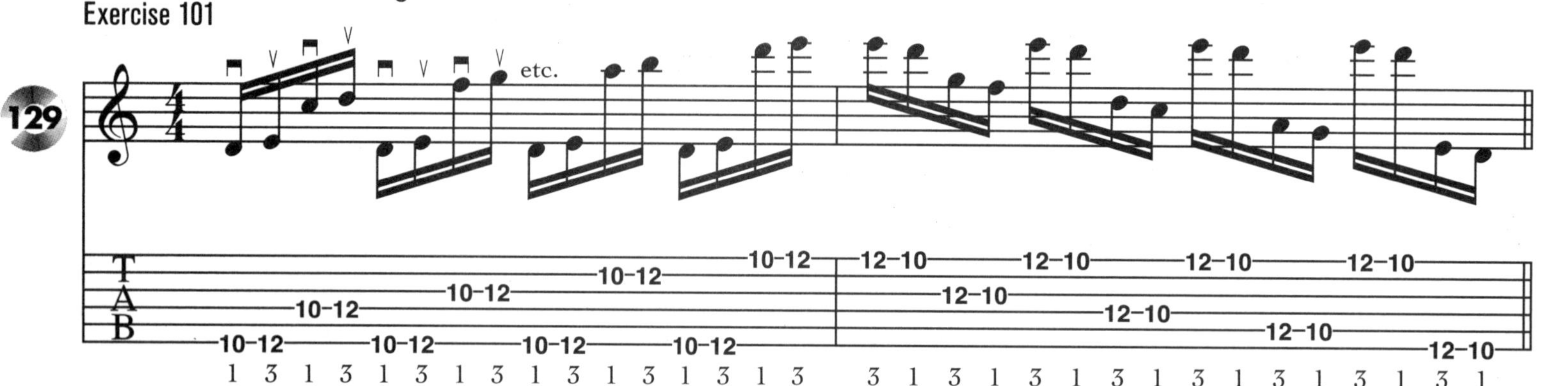

This passage arpeggiates an A Minor add 9 chord with string skipping and slides. It shows how string skipping can help to create a musical-sounding rhythm or lead riff.

Exercise 102

130

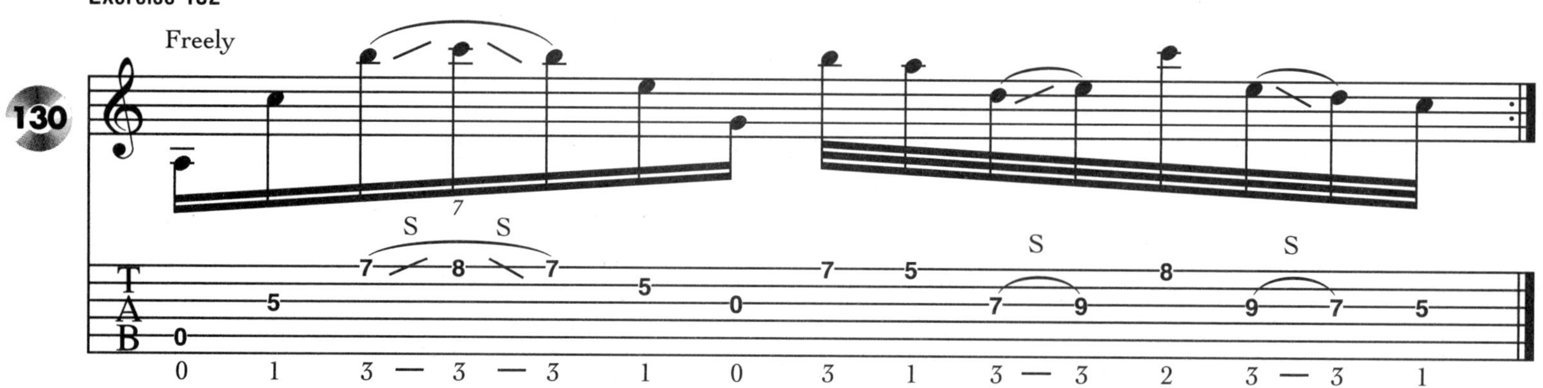

CHAPTER 20: ARPEGGIO ETUDES

Etude #1–Medieval Finger Torture

This monster sweep-picking etude connects all of the diatonic arpeggios in F Major with slides.
Pay close attention to the picking indications.

Exercise 103

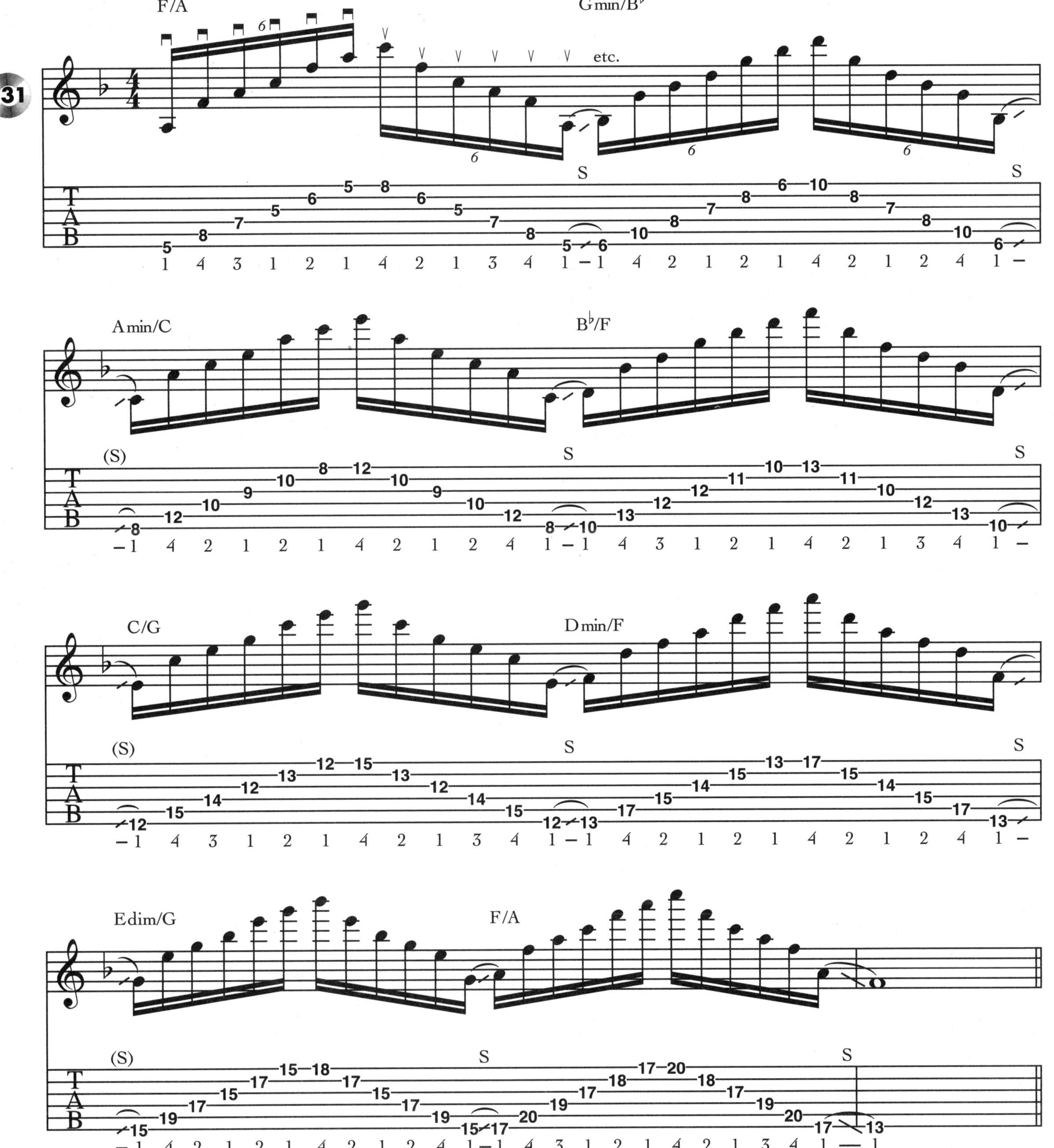

Etude #2–Human Sequencer Syndrome Etude

This etude features diatonic arpeggios and strummed chord forms in A Minor. It ends with a better than three-octave harmonic minor scale passage. Pay close attention to the pick strokes.

132 Exercise 104

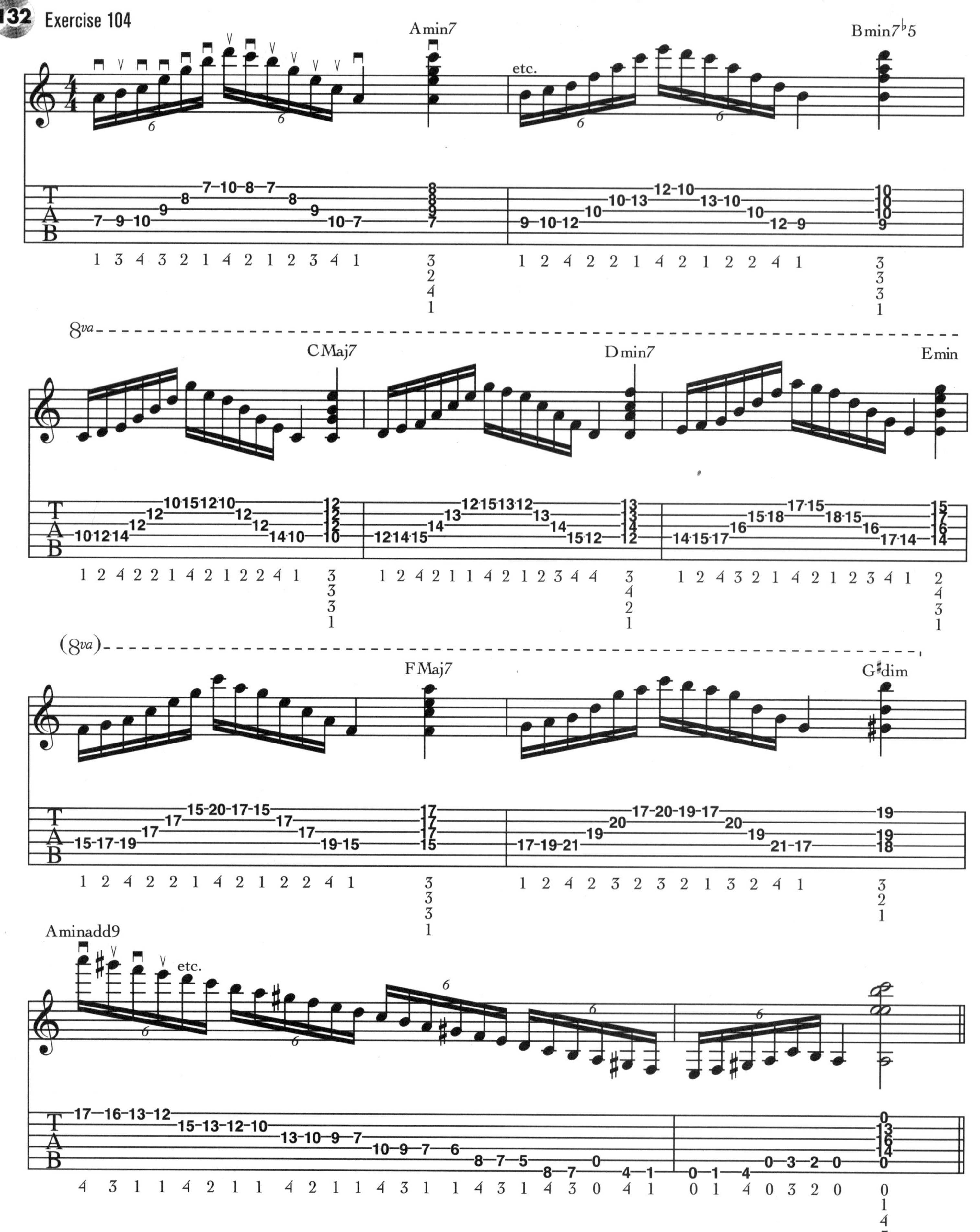

CHAPTER 21: "THE FLIGHT OF THE BUMBLEBEE"

This flamboyant piece of music was written in the Romantic period by the great Russian composer Rimsky-Korsakov. It is from the opera *The Legend of Tsar Saltan* and was originally penned for violin and orchestra. Here you will find it arranged for electric guitar solo (with someone playing the chords, it can also be a duet). It is the ultimate example of chromatic scales in action and is not only a beautiful piece of music but a very challenging speed-picking drill as well.

Many rock musicians have either toyed with this piece or actually performed it. The most authentic recorded rock guitar version is probably Jennifer Batten's completely finger-tapped rendition from her album *Above Below and Beyond*. Nuno Bettencourt of Extreme played around with it on *Pornograffiti*. There is also an amusing version called "Sting of the Bumblebee," played on eight-string bass guitar by the metal group Manowar. This tune presents such a challenge that there must be many more guitar versions floating around out there.

The version you will find here is very authentic. The only difference between this and the orchestral version is that it skips one repeat. In case you wish to perform it as a duet, the chords are shown below. Good luck!

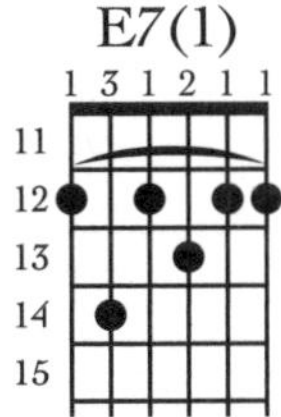
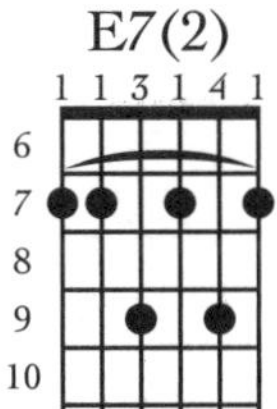
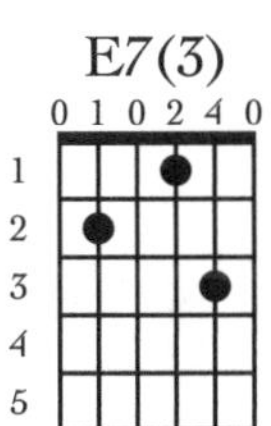
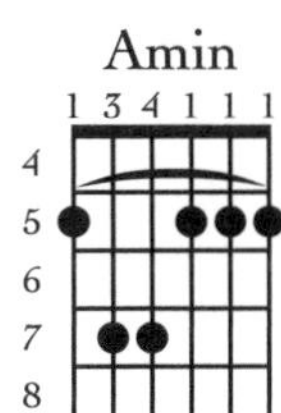
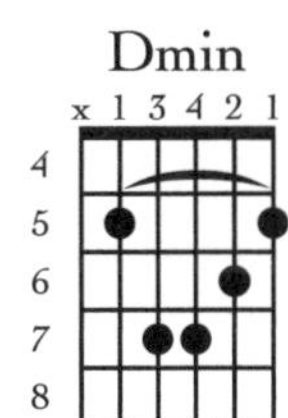
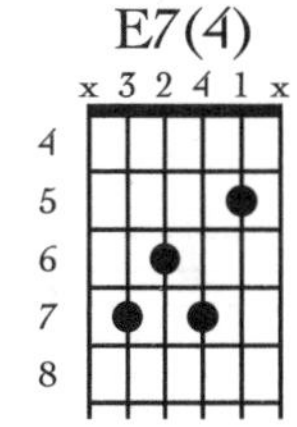

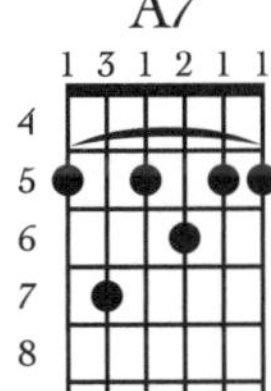
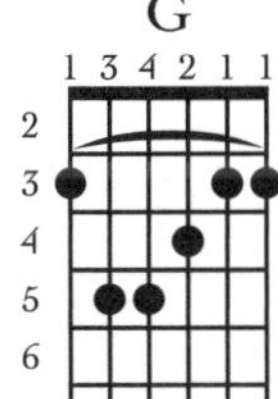
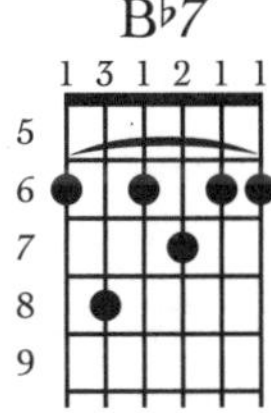
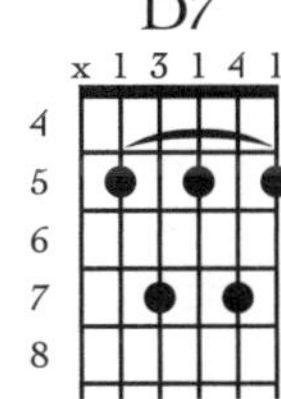
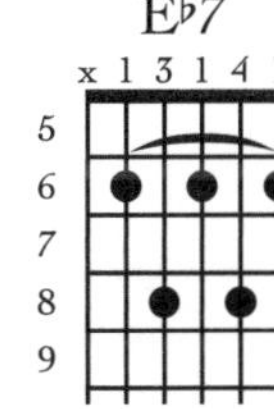
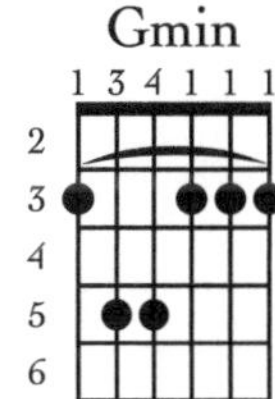

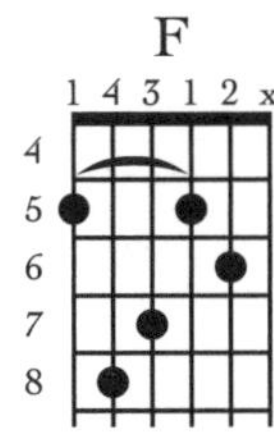
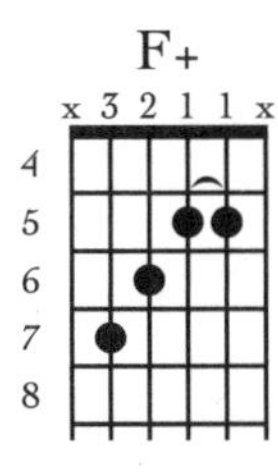
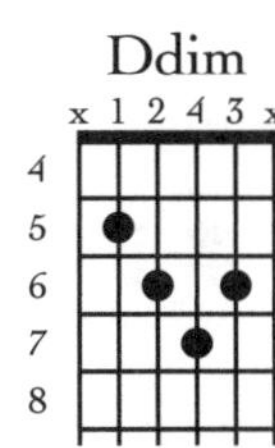
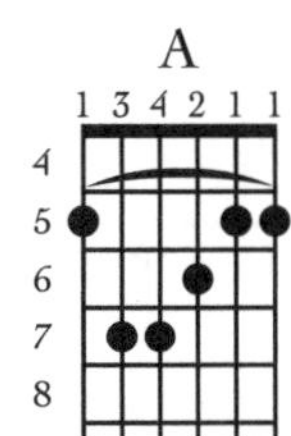

Exercise 105

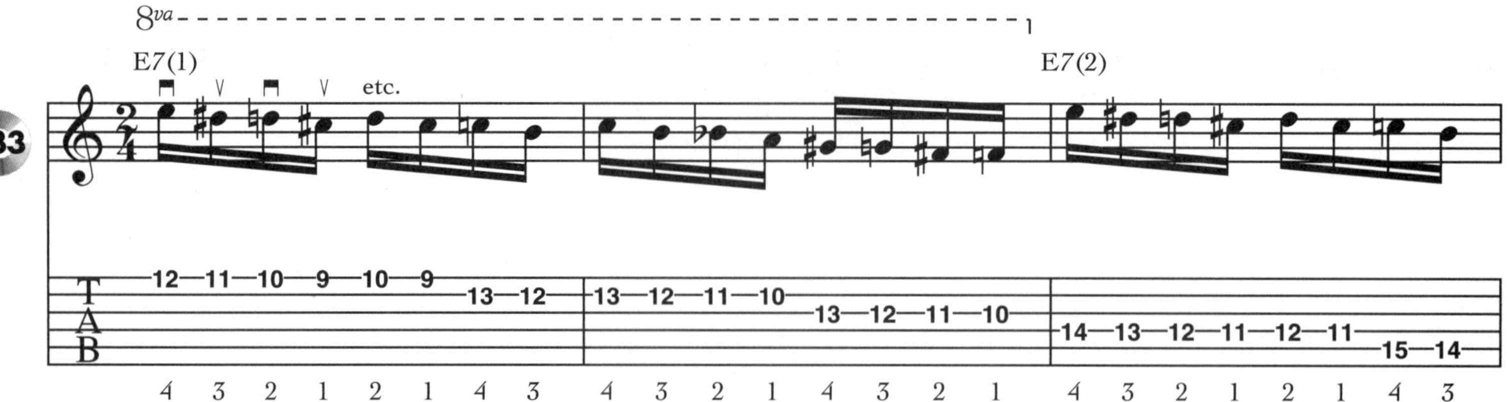

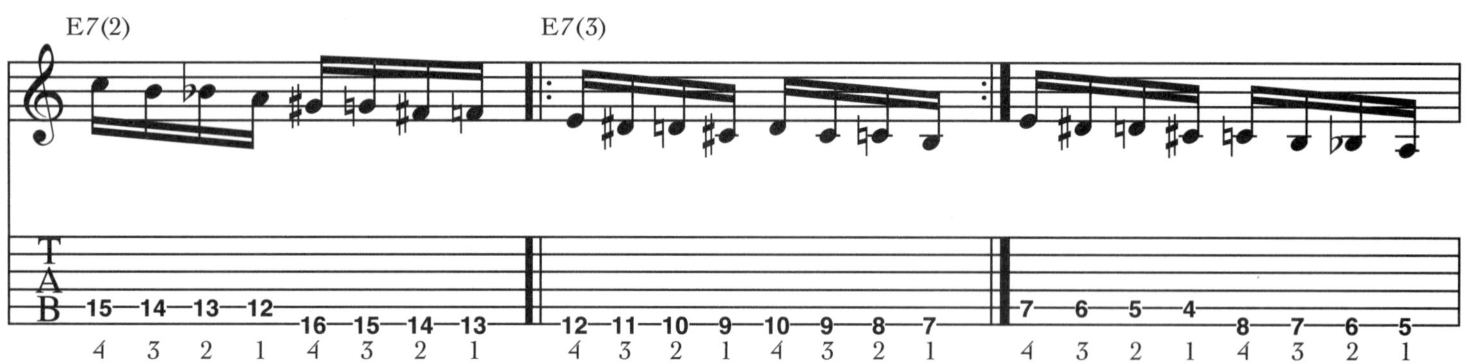

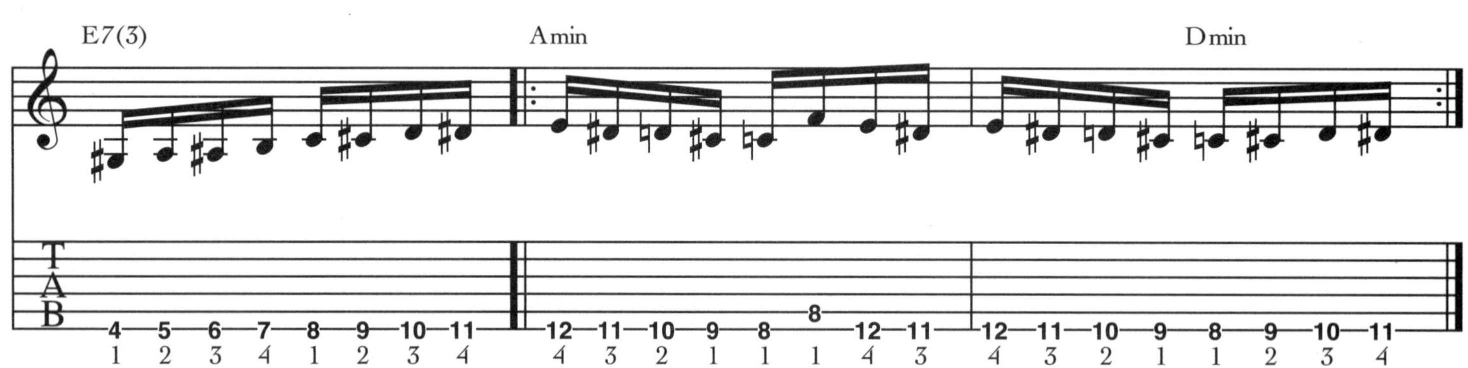

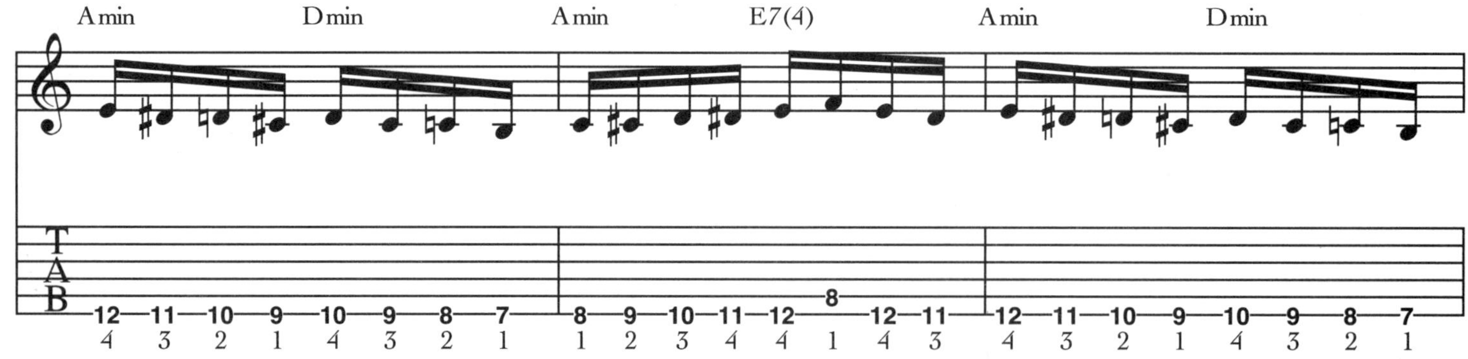

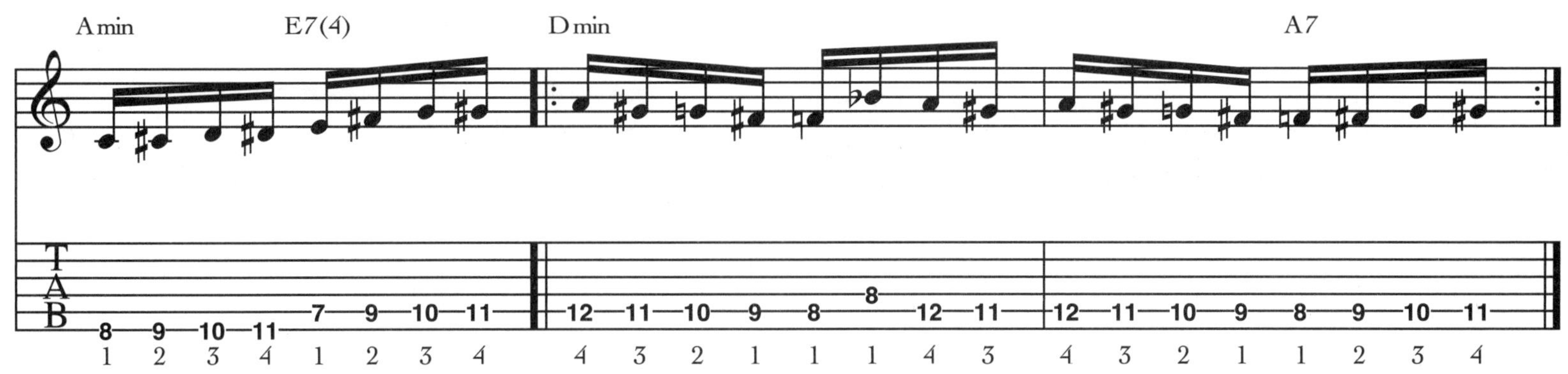
Amin   E7(4)   Dmin   A7

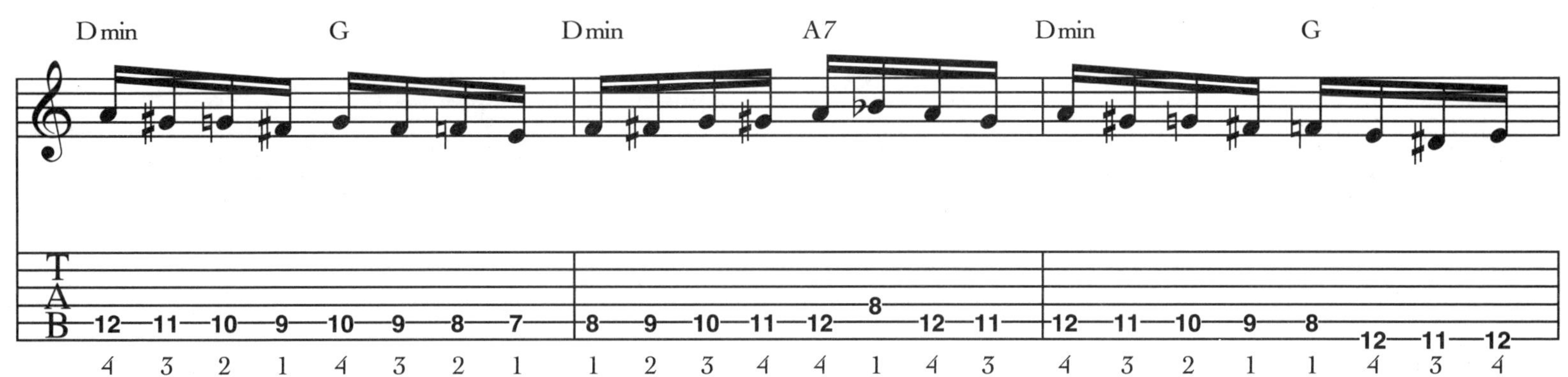
Dmin   G   Dmin   A7   Dmin   G

Dmin   A7   A7   B♭7
Nat. Harm.
P H P H P H P

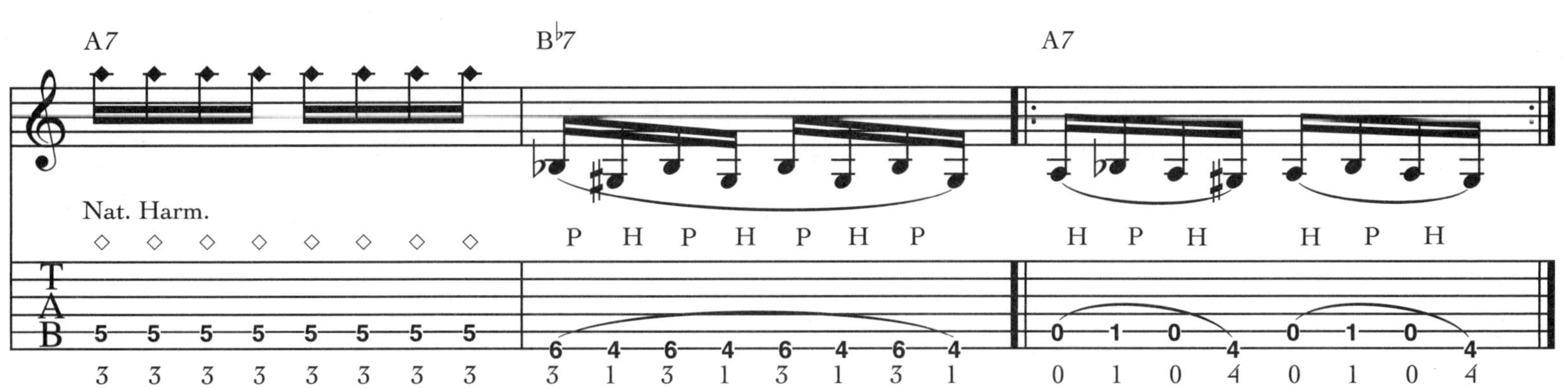
A7   B♭7   A7
Nat. Harm.
P H P H P H P   H P H   H P H

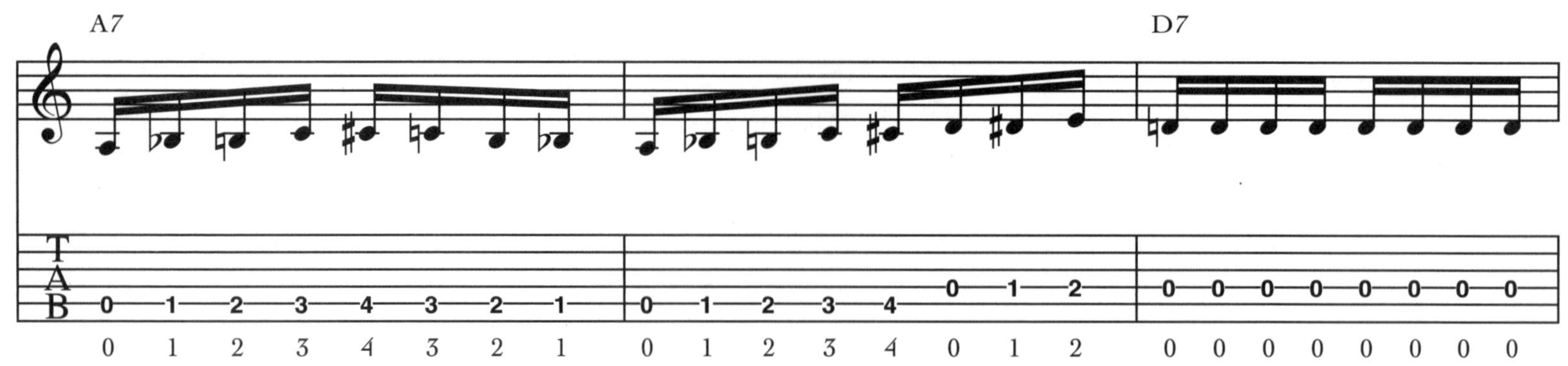
A7
D7
0 1 2 3 4 3 2 1   0 1 2 3 4 0 1 2   0 0 0 0 0 0 0 0

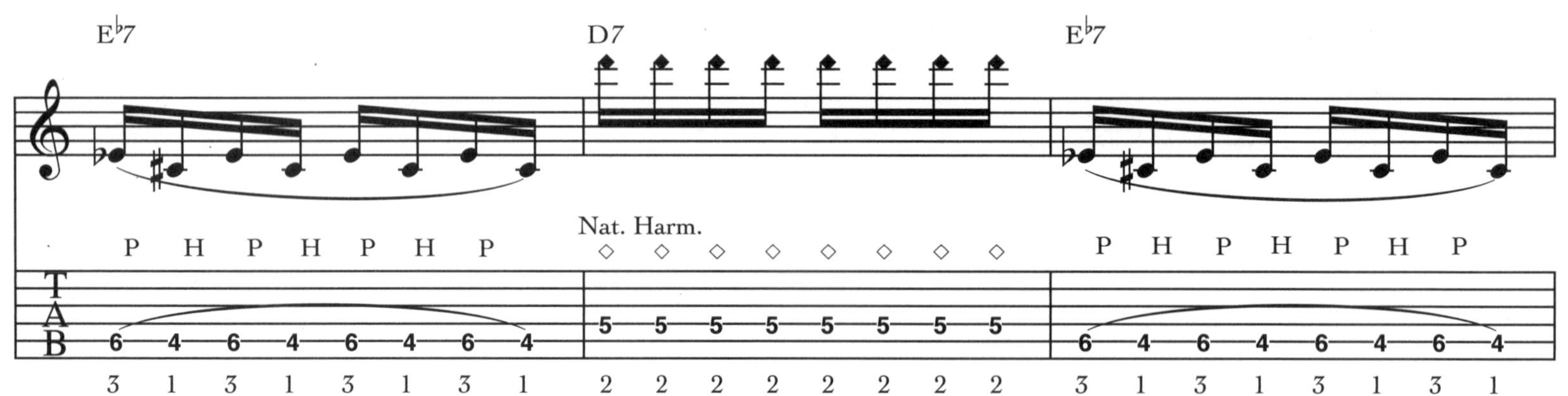
E♭7
D7
E♭7
P H P H P H P
Nat. Harm.
P H P H P H P
3 1 3 1 3 1 3 1   2 2 2 2 2 2 2 2   3 1 3 1 3 1 3 1

D7
H P H   H P H
0 1 0 4 0 1 0 4   0 1 2 3 4 3 2 1   0 1 2 3 1 2 3 4

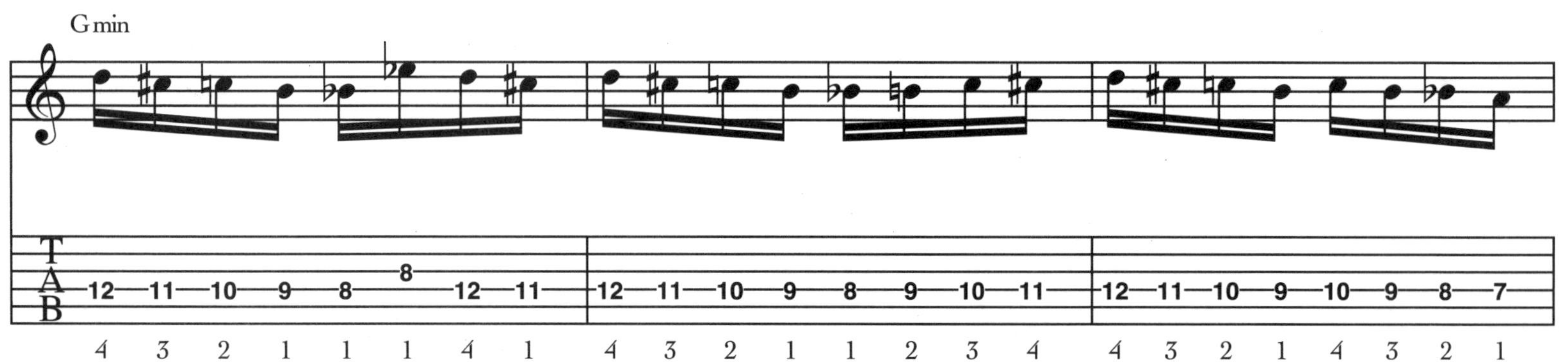
G min
4 3 2 1 1 1 4 1   4 3 2 1 1 2 3 4   4 3 2 1 4 3 2 1

Gmin
E7(4)
E7(4)
E5
8va
(Play 4 times)
Art. Harm.
(24)   (25)
H P H   H P H

(8va)
E5
(26) (26) (26) (25) (24)
Nat. Harm.
Nat. Harm.

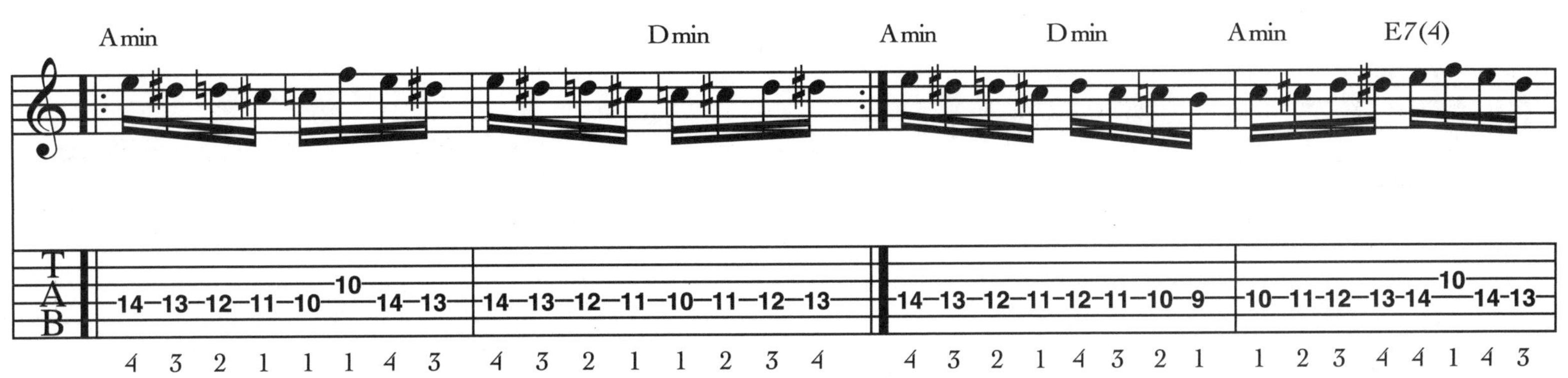

Amin
Dmin
Amin
Dmin
Amin
E7(4)

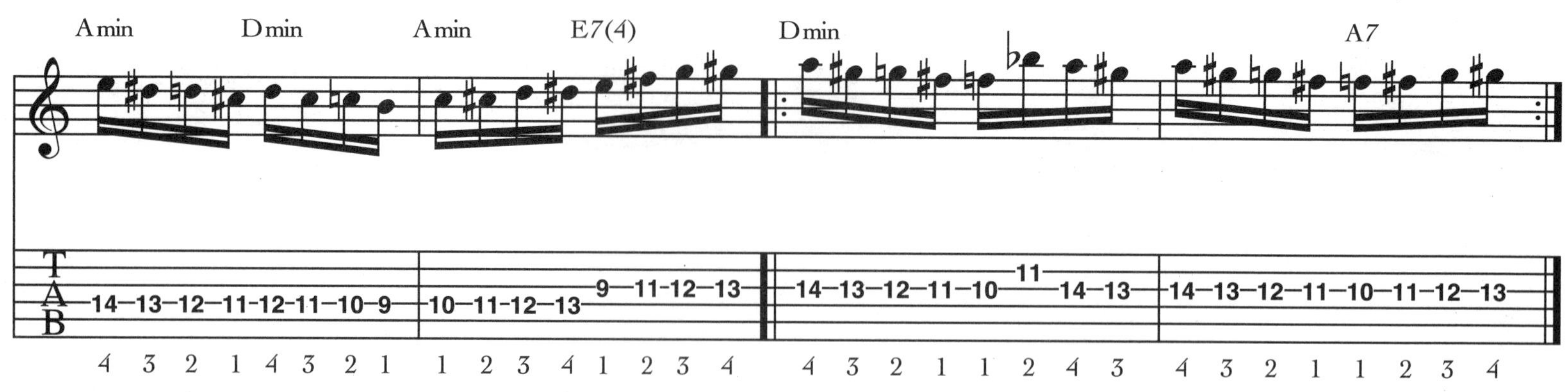

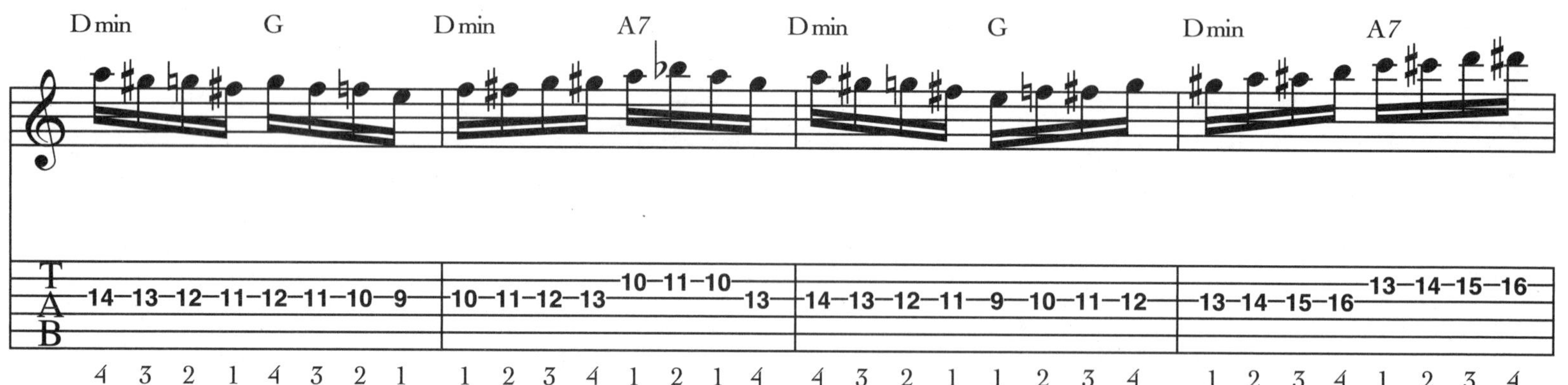

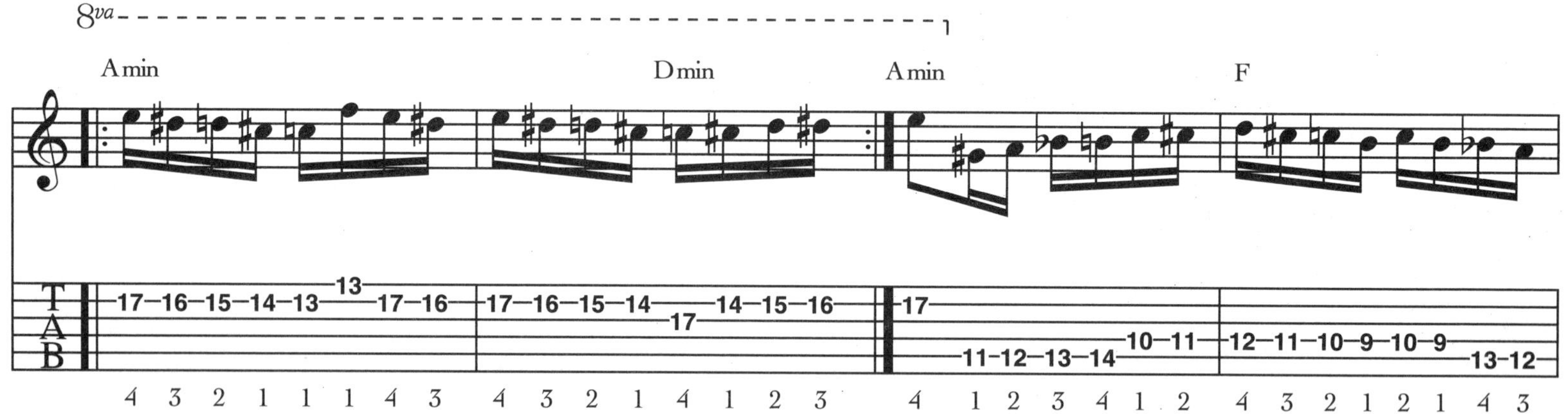

E+
Ddim
A
B♭7
A
H P H

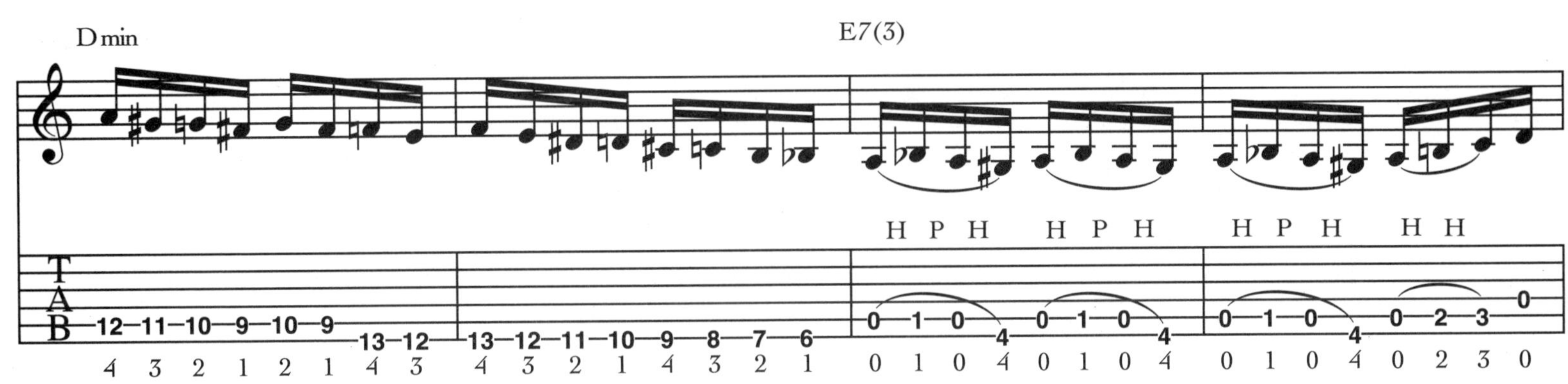
Dmin
E7(♭3)
H P H   H P H   H P H   H H

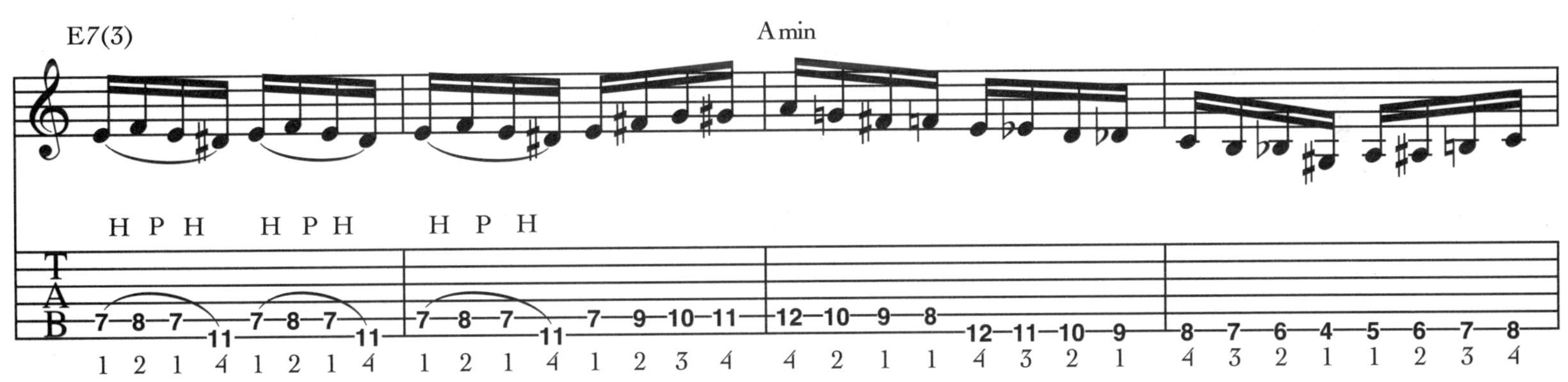
E7(♭3)
Amin
H P H   H P H   H P H

E7(♭3)
8va
Nat. Harm.
S

CHAPTER 22: SCALE FORMS

All of the scales in this index will be presented in five forms. The five basic chord forms, C, A, G, E, and D, form the nuclei of each scale in each five-form group. This is a very old system. Some call it the CAGED sequence. Joe Pass lectured about it for many years.

Here's how it works: Below you will see five forms of the minor pentatonic scale. Directly below each scale form you will see a grid with the corresponding chord form. Compare the diagrams to see how the notes line up. For clarity, the chord tones in the scales are gray.

Five Minor Pentatonic Scale Forms and Their Corresponding Chords

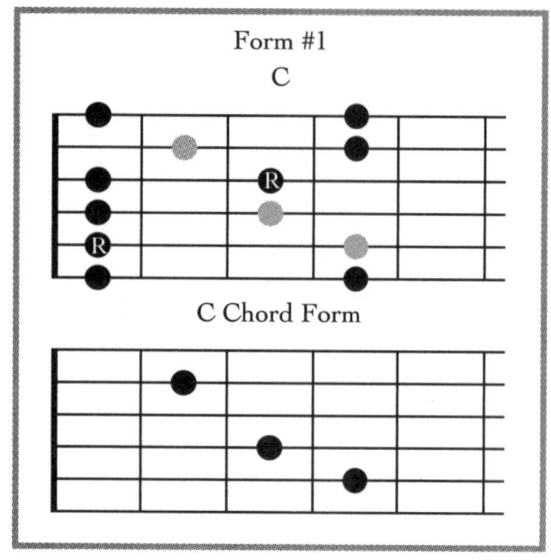

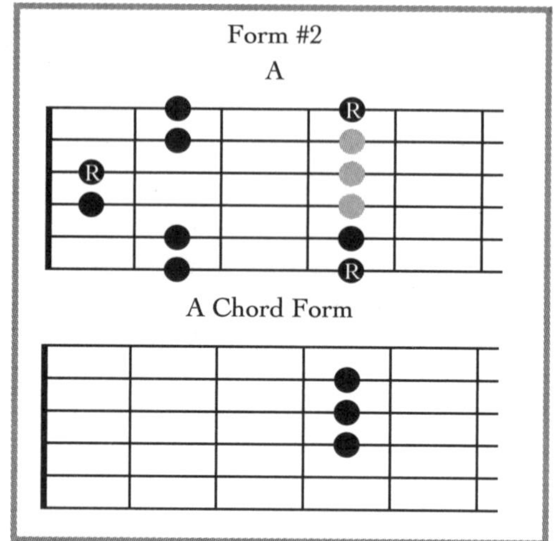

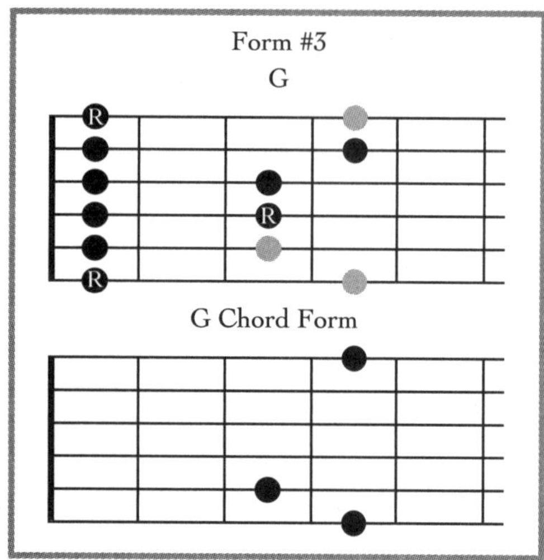

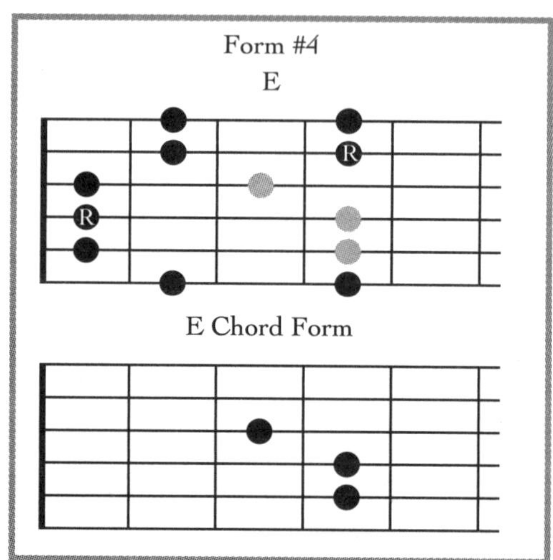

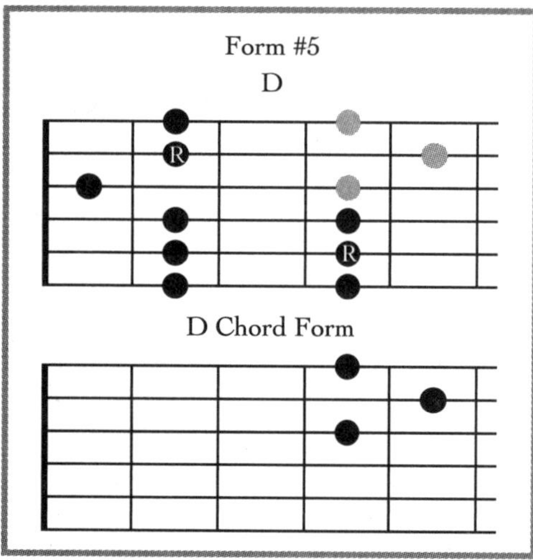

If you wish to climb the neck using any scale type, merely start each scale form's root note on the same letter name and sequence them in order: 1–2–3–4–5, or C–A–G–E–D. Form #1 will always correspond to the C chord. Form #2 will always correspond to the A chord, etc. Here is the A Minor Pentatonic scale sequenced up the neck in this manner:

The A Minor Pentatonic Scale

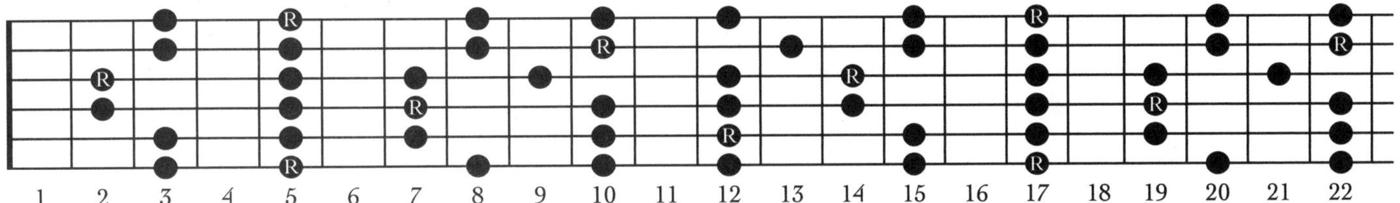

The same logic applies to all of the scale forms that follow in this index.

The Major Scale

Form #1 (C)

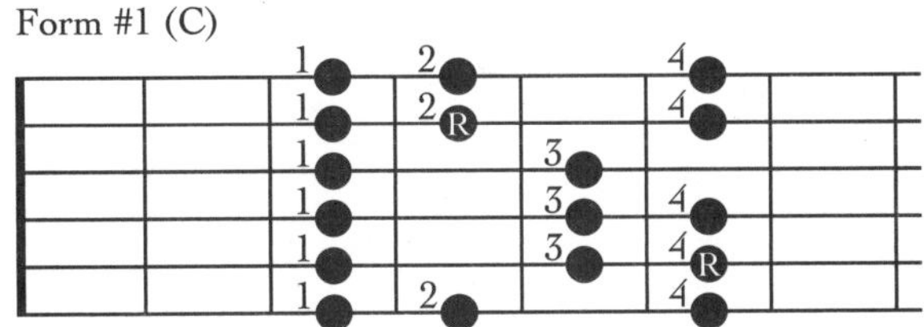

Form #2 (A)

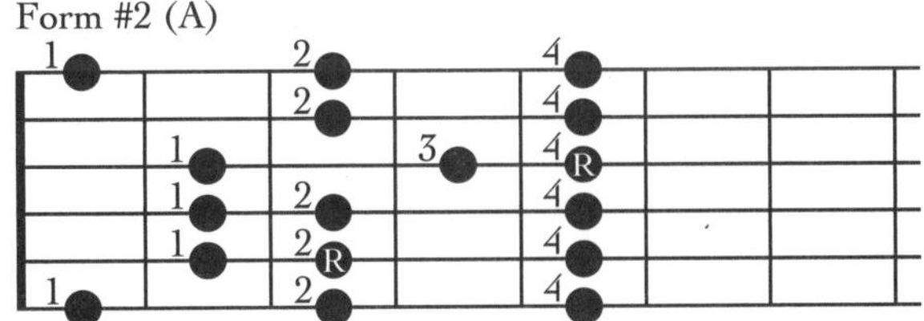

Form #3 (G)

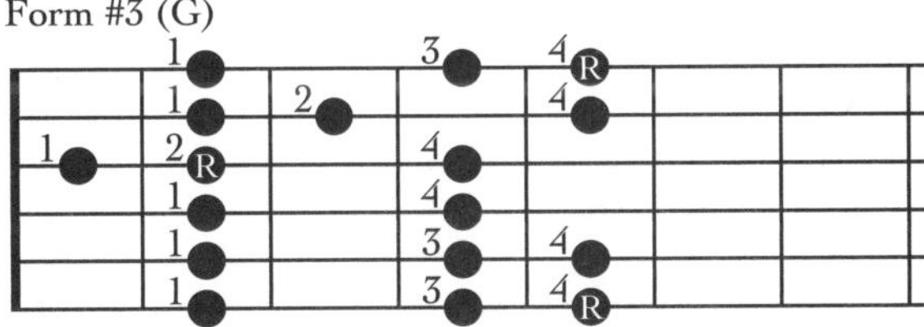

Form #4 (E)

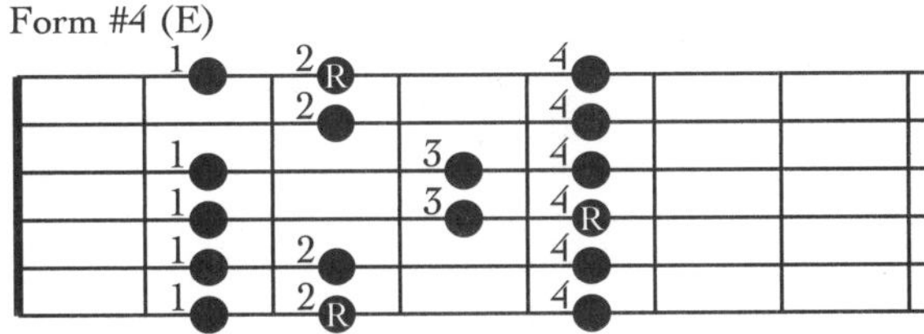

Form #5 (D)

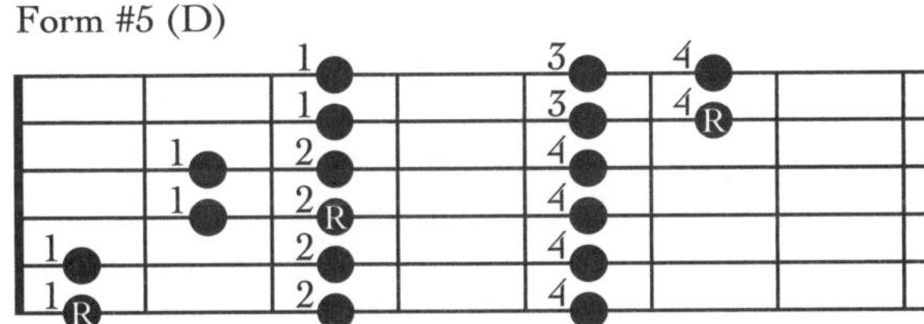

The A Major Scale

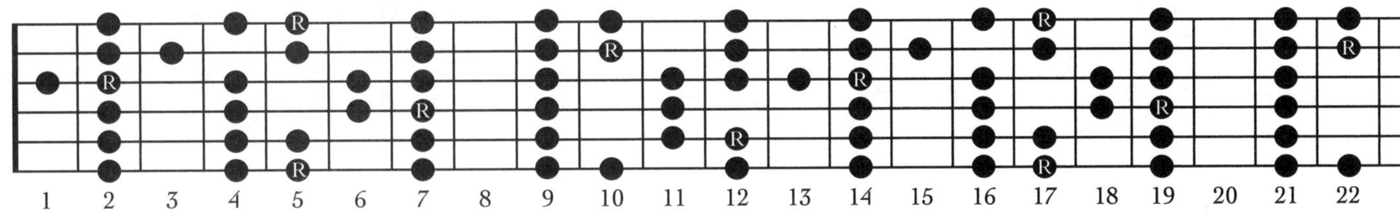

The Harmonic Minor Scale

Form #1 (C)

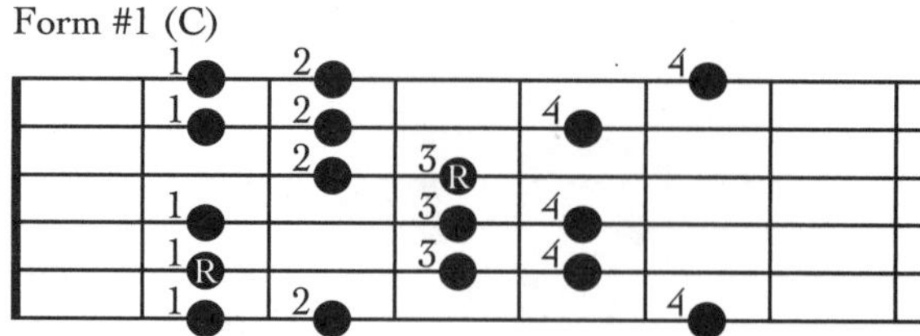

Form #2 (A)

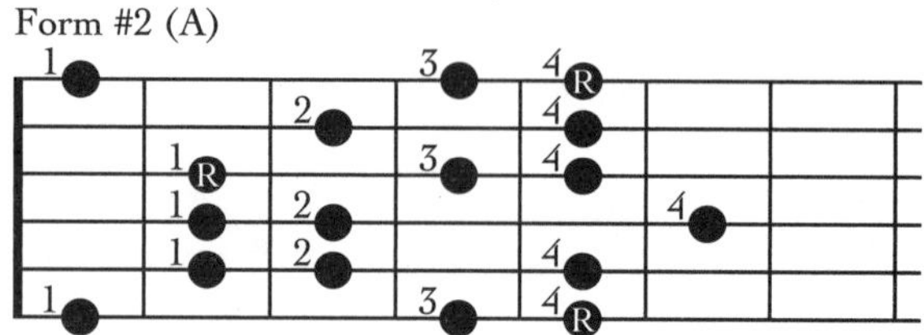

Form #3 (G)

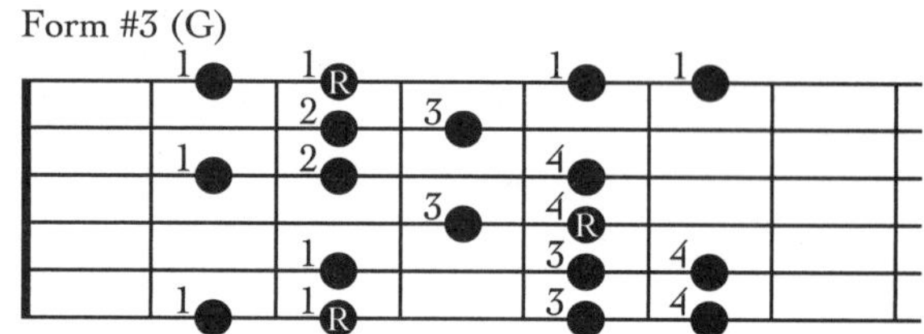

Form #4 (E)

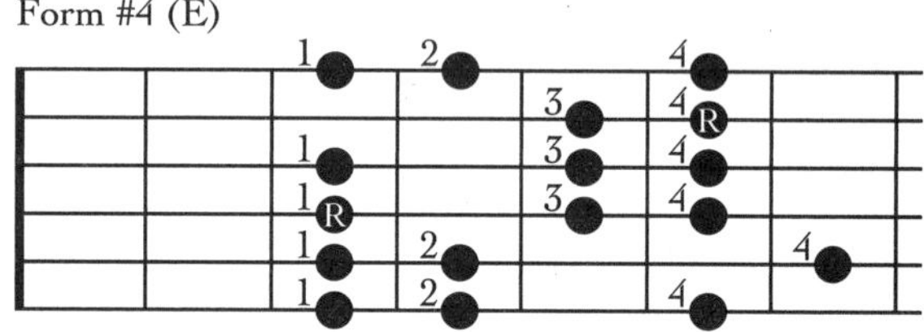

Form #5 (D)

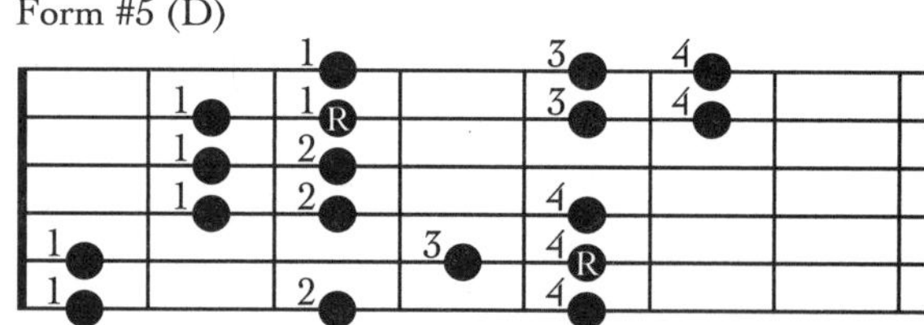

The A Harmonic Minor Scale

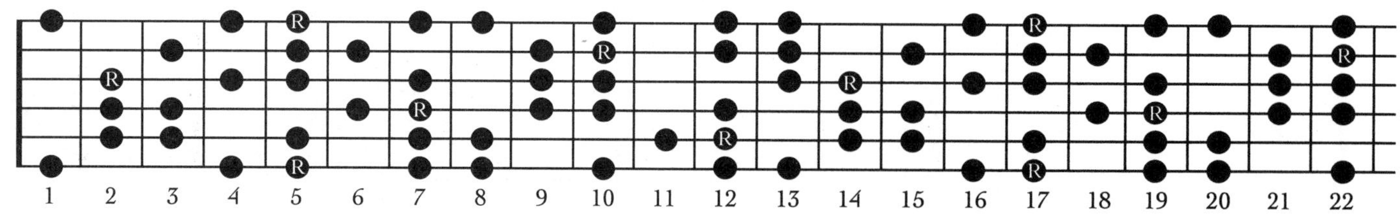

The Major Pentatonic Scale

Form #1 (C)

Form #2 (A)

Form #3 (G)

Form #4 (E)

Form #5 (D)

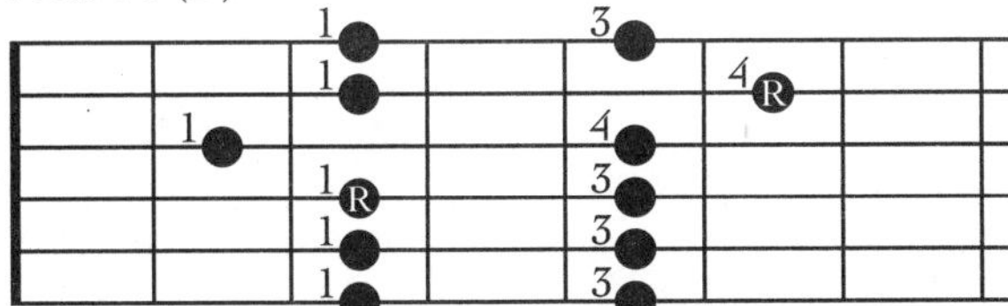

The A Major Pentatonic Scale

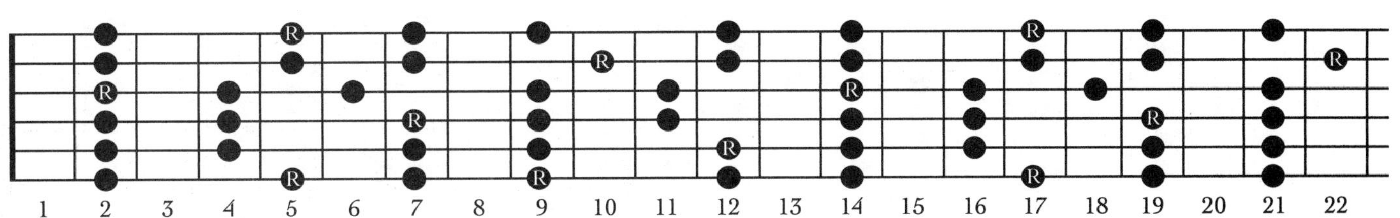

The Blues Scale

Form #1 (C)

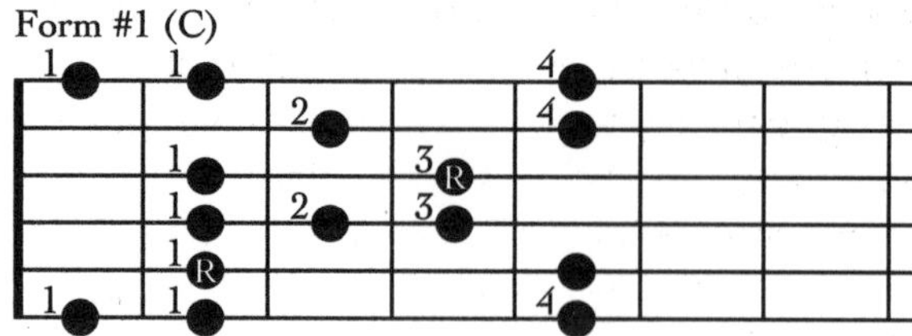

Form #2 (A)

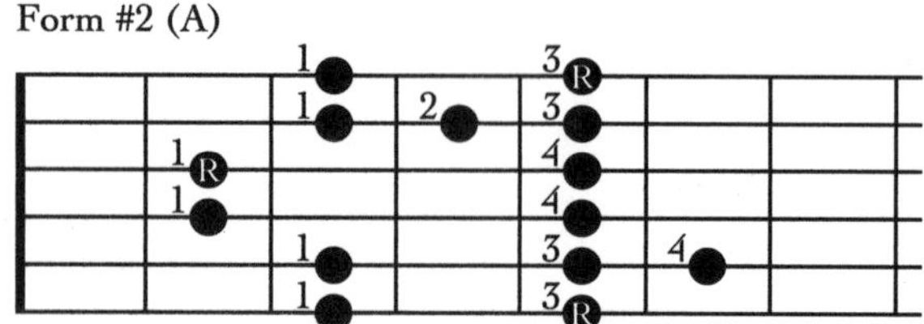

Form #3 (G)

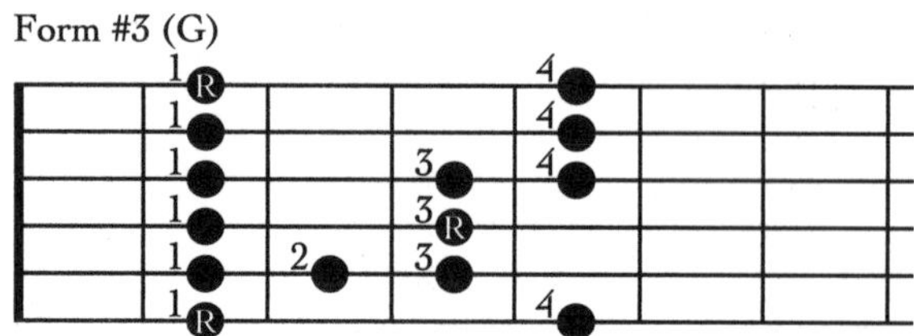

Form #4 (E)

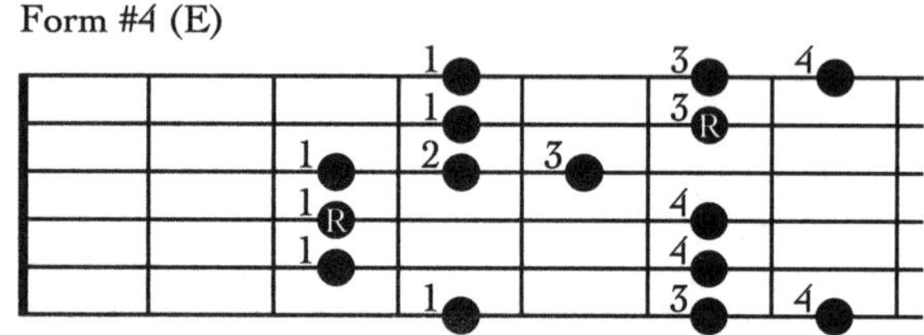

Form #5 (D)

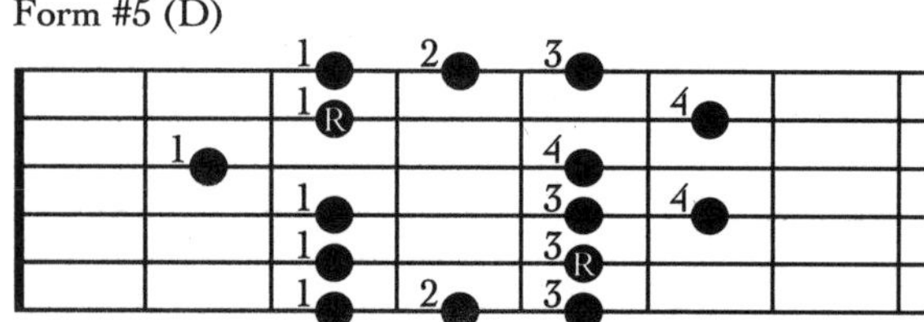

The A Blues Scale

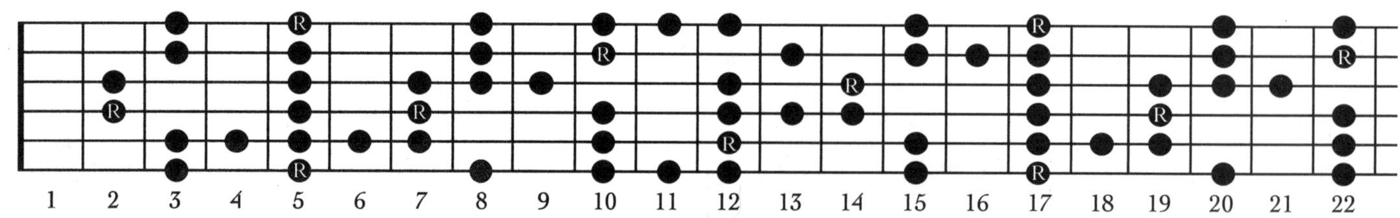

The Modes of the Major Scale

We can create seven different scales from any major scale simply by playing it starting on each of the seven different tones. These are called *modes*. The names may sound a bit strange because they are classical Greek words referring to specific regions in the Mediterranean area. In order, the modes of the major scale are as follows: 1—Ionian, 2—Dorian, 3—Phrygian, 4—Lydian, 5—Mixolydian, 6—Aeolian, and 7—Locrian. You don't need to learn any more scale forms in order to be able to play all seven modes in any key. The five major scale forms found earlier in this chapter are all you need.

The diagram below shows how the modes work in the key of C Major. Of course, the same concepts can be applied to any other key.

C-D-E-F-G-A-B-C...C Ionian (The same as C Major)

  D-E-F-G-A-B-C-D... D Dorian

    E-F-G-A-B-C-D-E.................................... E Phrygian

      F-G-A-B-C-D-E-F................................. F Lydian

        G-A-B-C-D-E-F-G............................. G Mixolydian

          A-B-C-D-E-F-G-A........................... A Aeolian (The same as A Natural Minor)

            B-C-D-E-F-G-A-B....................... B Locrian

All you need to do to play any given mode is to start one of the major scale forms on a note other than its root. Some examples are given below. The first note of the mode becomes the root of the mode.

A Aeolian—The 6th Mode of the C Major

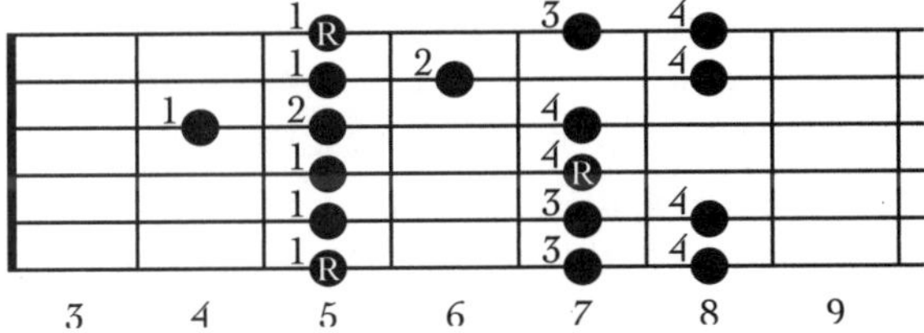

B Phrygian—The 3rd Mode of the G Major

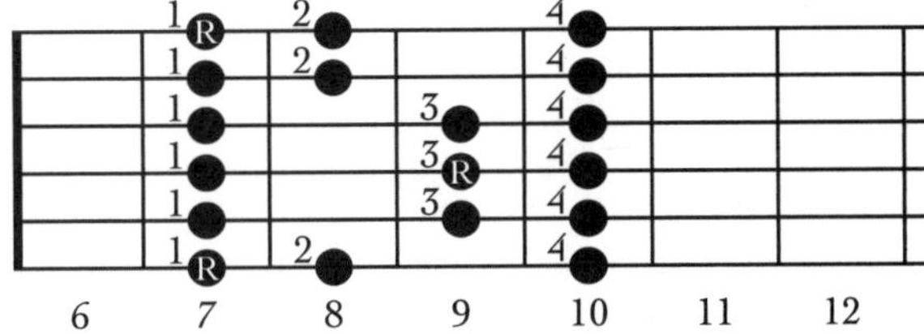

G Mixolydian—The 5th Mode of the C Major

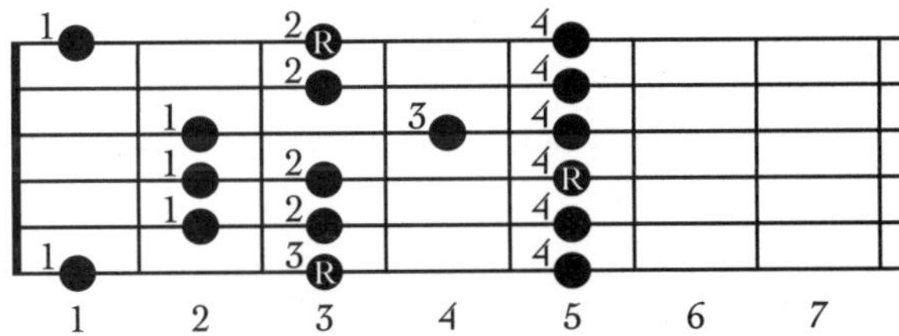

D♯ Locrian—The 7th Mode of the E Major

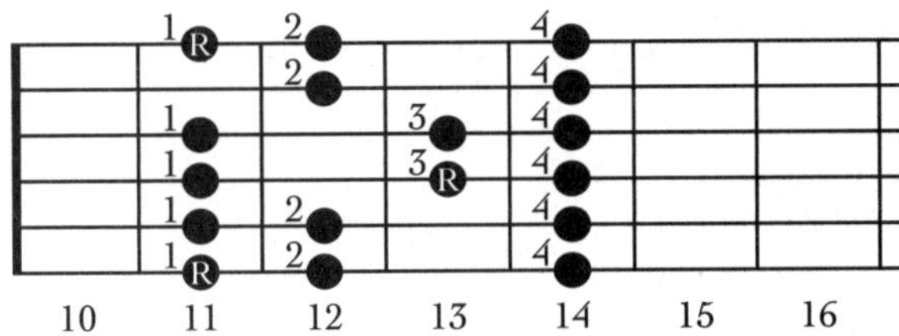

FINAL THOUGHTS

Well, here we are, on the last page of *The Serious Guitarist: Rock Chops*. At this point, you owe yourself a great big pat on the back for making it through. I know it hasn't been easy. Much of this material is very challenging, even for me, and I wrote the book! How about that arrangement of "Flight of the Bumblebee?" But just think—now you can even shred for your grandmother without giving her a heart attack!

Writing this book has been a labor of love for me. I've always wanted to create a book which demystifies rock lead guitar. After decades of playing, here it is. But, it's not really over until I leave you with a few more pieces of fortune-cookie wisdom for the road. So, here it goes!

- Don't let technique "run away with you." Play from the heart. Don't let your music become a random by-product of technique.

- Practice soloing in two different ways: 1) improvise, 2) compose (work them out in advance). Listen with an ear for whether a solo is improvised, composed, or both.

- Start slowly. Build intensity as you solo. Tell a story with your music.

- Don't judge yourself against others. Judge yourself against your own potential. How close are you to reaching it?

- Listen closely to yourself when you play. You can't fix problems if you don't know they exist.

- While jamming, listen closely to the people you play with. You can't support them musically if you don't know what they're doing.

- Listen closely to great music. Absorbing the styles of others will help you create your own unique style. The list of 15 songs that you'll find on the following page are all from the rock genre, be they fusion, Southern, classic, shred, metal, funk, or blues. These songs, and the guitar solos in them, are all shining examples of rock guitar excellence. They each have different lessons to teach and have been great inspirations to me over the years. I strongly suggest that you listen to, and study, each of them.

Listening List

Another Brick in the Wall, Part 2	Pink Floyd
Black Star	Yngwie Malmsteen
Crazy Train	Ozzy Osbourne
Eruption	Van Halen
For the Love of God	Steve Vai
Killing in the Name	Rage Against the Machine
Maggot Brain (live)	P-Funk
Mediterranean Sundance (live)	Di Meola, McLaughlin, De Lucia
That Smell	Lynyrd Skynyrd
School Days	Stanley Clarke
Scuttle Buttin'	Stevie Ray Vaughan
Spanish Fly	Van Halen
Stairway to Heaven	Led Zeppelin
Unaccompanied solo at Woodstock	Jimi Hendrix
Zomby Woof	Frank Zappa